Dedications

First and foremost, I want to extend my heartfelt thanks to each and every one of you who has purchased this book. Your support means the world to me, and I'm honored to be part of your journey toward financial empowerment.
I wish you all the best as you apply the strategies and insights shared in these pages. If you take the action to implement what you've learned, there's no doubt in my mind that you can improve your financial future
starting today and continuing well into the years ahead.
Remember, investments and success aren't about luck; they are about action. Every successful person you admire reached their level of achievement because they took consistent, focused action. It's as simple as that. If you take action, you can absolutely reach the destination you desire.
And always keep in mind: time is your most valuable asset. Unlike money, possessions, or anything else, time is something you can never get back. So use it wisely, invest in your growth, and never waste a moment of it. The future you want is built in the present.
Thank you for believing in this journey, and here's to your future success!

Most importantly To my Daughter, My one and only,
It has been an incredible journey watching you grow into the remarkable woman you are today. From teaching you about money, business, and the key elements of success, to sharing countless cherished moments together
Every step of the way has been a blessing. I am so proud of all you've accomplished and all the greatness that lies ahead for you.
Thank you for everything you've done for me, for your unwavering love, and for the joy you bring into my life. I treasure the best times we've shared, and I look forward to so many more in the future.
Though you've grown up so quickly, know that you will always be my little girl.
Always take care of your mom, and don't forget to look after Orange and Daisy too.
I know you'll continue to do great things
never stop believing in yourself. I will always be proud of your Accomplishments
With all my love, Dad

To my parents,
Thank you for everything you did for me, for all the great moments we shared in my life, and for the opportunities you gave me to grow into the person I am today. I hope that wherever you are now, you have found peace. Until we meet again, know that you will always be with me in spirit.

To Bob,
You were like a second father to me and You're a legend in my mind and in the minds of anyone lucky enough to have shared a moment with you. You taught me so much, and the memories we created together are treasures I will carry forever. The adventures we had well, that's another story for another time. I hope you've found your peace, and know that I will never forget the lessons and laughter you brought into my life.

To my brother, his wonderful wife, and my amazing niece thank you for always being there for me through thick and thin. From Bobby's wild camping trip at Jones Lake to the most recent unforgettable adventure where the bear stole my burgers (she won that round, I guess), you've made every moment special. I'll forever cherish the laughter, the stories, and the memories we've created together.

That same night under the vast sky in complete awe of the Milky Way above I will never forget how vibrant the Milky way was that night, with the city's lights far behind us, was nothing short of magical.

To my friends and family,
You have all been incredible people to grow up with and share life's journey. A few of you may be a little crazy (in the best way), but you've each brought something truly special to my world. From the wild adventures to the quiet moments, I've had some of the most amazing times with you, and for that, I'll always be grateful.

To my buddy Mike,
Another legend in my mind. You taught me so much, and I'm forever thankful for your wisdom and friendship. I hope you are at peace now, wherever you are. Like so many others on this list, you left us far too soon. You've taught me that life is short, and time is the most precious gift we have. I'll carry that lesson with me always.

To everyone who has supported me along this journey — thank you. Your love, guidance, and presence have shaped me more than you'll ever know. I carry a piece of all of you with me in everything I do.

Disclaimer

This book is intended solely for educational purposes and aims to provide knowledge about the future of the changing economy. It offers insights on how individuals can adapt to upcoming economic shifts and work with these changes to create a better future for themselves.

The contents of this book are not to be construed as financial or investment advice. The author and publisher make no guarantees regarding any financial outcomes or the effectiveness of the strategies outlined. Any actions taken based on the information provided in this book are done so at the reader's own risk.

The author and publisher assume no responsibility for any investment gains or losses, or any other financial outcomes, that result from the use of the information in this book. The purpose of this book is to serve as a step-by-step guide for taking action and implementing ideas aimed at making money and securing financial success in the future. However, individual results will vary and depend on many factors outside the scope of this work.

Always seek advice from a qualified financial professional before making any investment decisions.

Introduction

Chapter 1
The Changing Landscape of Wealth in 2025

Chapter 2
The Gig Economy and Freelancing Revolution

Chapter 3
Building Passive Income Streams

Chapter 4
Emerging Investment Opportunities: AI, Crypto, and Beyond

Chapter 5
The Future of E-Commerce and Online Business

Chapter 6
Becoming a Content Creator: Monetizing Your Passion

Chapter 7
Building a Future-Proof Career with AI and Automation

Chapter 8
The Importance of Networking and Building Relationships

Section 1 Digital Entrepreneurship & Online Businesses

Chapter 9
Start a YouTube Channel

Chapter 10
Create an Online Course

Chapter 11
Launch an E-commerce Store

Chapter 12
How to Develop a Mobile App: A Step-by-Step Guide

Chapter 13
How to Sell NFTs (Non-Fungible Tokens): A Step-by-Step Guide

Chapter 14
Affiliate Marketing

Chapter 15

Virtual Consulting or Coaching

Chapter 16
Create a Subscription Service or Membership Site

Chapter 17
How to Create a Subscription Service or Membership Site

Chapter 18
Start a Podcast

Section 2. Tech-driven Opportunities

Chapter 19
AI & Chatbot Development

Chapter 20
Data Science & Analytics

Chapter 21
Cybersecurity Services

Chapter 22
Software as a Service (SaaS)

Chapter 23
3D Printing Business

Chapter 24
16. Tech Support for Small Businesses

Chapter 25
Drone Services

Chapter 26
Virtual Reality Experiences

Chapter 27
Blockchain Development

Chapter 28
Cloud Computing Services

Section 3. Sustainable Ventures

Chapter 29
Eco-Friendly Product Design

Chapter 30
Green Energy Consulting

Chapter 31
Upcycled & Repurposed Goods

Chapter 32
Urban Farming & Vertical Gardens

Chapter 33
Electric Vehicle (EV) Charging Stations

Chapter 34
Eco-Friendly Landscaping

Chapter 35
Carbon Offset Programs

Chapter 36
Green Building & Design

Chapter 37
Plastic-Free Product Line

Chapter 38
Water Conservation Solutions

Section 4 Gig Economy & Freelancing

Chapter 39
Freelance Writing or Copywriting

Chapter 40
Graphic Design or Illustration

Chapter 41
Virtual Assistant Services

Chapter 42
Social Media Management

Chapter 43
Online Tutoring or Teaching

Chapter 44
Website Development

Chapter 45
Influencer Marketing

Chapter 46
Event Planning & Coordination

Chapter 47
Delivery and Ride-Sharing

Chapter 48
Pet Sitting or Dog Walking

Section 5. Investing & Passive Income

Chapter 49
Real Estate Investment

Chapter 50
Dividend Investing

Chapter 51
Peer-to-Peer Lending

Chapter 52
Buy & Sell Domain Names

Chapter 53
Rent Out Property on Airbnb

Chapter 54
How to Start an Investment Business in Cryptocurrencies

Chapter 55
Create a Print-on-Demand Store

Chapter 56
Start a Crowdfunding Campaign

**Chapter 57
Venture into Angel Investing**

**Chapter 58
Start a Vending Machine Business**

This book is about the best ways of making money in 2025 and beyond. The world of work, investment, and entrepreneurship is changing rapidly, driven by technological advancements, shifts in consumer behavior, and new economic models. The chapters in this book will cover different aspects of earning money from now into the future.

Chapter 1

Introduction - The Changing Landscape of Wealth in 2025

In this opening chapter, we will provide an overview of how the ways people earn and grow wealth have evolved over the past few decades and what the future holds. We'll focus on major trends driving these changes and introduce the different strategies readers can use to make money in 2025 and beyond.

Key Themes:

- **The Digital Revolution:** Technology has already changed how we work, and by 2025, the reliance on digital tools, automation, and artificial intelligence will be greater than ever.

- **Remote Work & Globalization:** The rise of remote work and global freelancing platforms will continue to open up opportunities for earning income from anywhere.

- **The Shift Toward Sustainability:** Growing environmental consciousness is driving demand for sustainable products and services, creating new revenue streams.

- **Decentralized Finance:** Blockchain and cryptocurrency technologies are reshaping the way people invest, bank, and transfer money.

Chapter 2

The Gig Economy and Freelancing Revolution

Freelancing, consulting, and gig work are expected to dominate the labor market in 2025. With advancements in automation, AI, and digital tools, the demand for specialized services will continue to rise.

Key Themes:

- **Freelance Platforms:** How platforms like Upwork, Fiverr, and Freelancer are revolutionizing the job market.

- **Skill Development:** The most in-demand skills for freelancers, including digital marketing, web development, AI training, and content creation.

- **Building a Personal Brand:** How to market yourself in a crowded online space and create long-term client relationships.

- **Remote Work Strategies:** How to effectively work and thrive in a remote environment, including tips for productivity, communication, and work-life balance.

Actionable Advice:
- How to find clients online and build a reputation.
- The benefits of diversifying your client base and specializing in high-demand niches.
- Tools to streamline your workflow and enhance your productivity as a remote worker.

Chapter 3

Building Passive Income Streams

While active work is often necessary to earn money, the true wealth-building strategies for 2025 will involve creating passive income. This chapter will explore the various ways people can create ongoing income with less active involvement.

Key Themes:

- Real Estate Crowdfunding: As real estate becomes increasingly expensive, platforms like Fundrise and RealtyMogul are enabling individuals to invest in real estate with low capital.

- Dividend Stocks and ETFs: Low-risk investments in dividend-paying stocks or exchange-traded funds that can generate passive income.

- Intellectual Property and Royalties: Writing books, creating courses, or producing music that generates royalties over time.

- Automated Online Businesses: Building and automating e-commerce stores, subscription services, and affiliate marketing ventures.

Actionable Advice:
- How to start small with passive income investments and scale over time.
- How to use technology to automate business processes, freeing up time for other ventures.
- Examples of successful passive income strategies, from blogs to online courses.

Chapter 4

Emerging Investment Opportunities: AI, Crypto, and Beyond

By 2025, traditional investment opportunities will continue to evolve, and new asset classes are emerging that offer significant potential for growth. This chapter will cover how to take advantage of these new investment opportunities.

Key Themes:

- Cryptocurrencies and Blockchain: Beyond Bitcoin and Ethereum, we'll explore how blockchain technology will disrupt various sectors, including finance, healthcare, and logistics.

- AI-Driven Investing: AI tools that allow everyday investors to leverage advanced algorithms for better stock picks and market predictions.

- Green & Sustainable Investments: The rise of green bonds, clean energy stocks, and sustainable ETFs as consumers and companies prioritize sustainability.

- Crowdfunding and Peer-to-Peer Lending: How platforms like Kickstarter, GoFundMe, and lending platforms are democratizing investment.

Actionable Advice:
- How to start investing in cryptocurrencies safely and responsibly.
- Understanding the potential and risks of investing in AI and technology companies.
- How to evaluate and pick sustainable investment opportunities.

Chapter 5

The Future of E-Commerce and Online Business

The digital marketplace will continue to grow, with new trends in e-commerce shaping the way people buy and sell. This chapter will focus on how to build and grow an online business in 2025.

Key Themes:

- **Direct-to-Consumer (DTC) Brands:** How new companies are cutting out the middleman and building profitable brands by selling directly to consumers via their websites or platforms like Shopify.

- **Subscription Models:** The rise of subscription services that offer recurring revenue, from digital content to niche products.

- **AI-Powered E-Commerce:** How AI is transforming the customer experience with personalized recommendations, chatbots, and smart inventory management.

- **Social Commerce:** Leveraging platforms like Instagram, TikTok, and YouTube to sell products directly to followers.

Actionable Advice:
- How to find profitable niches and design an e-commerce strategy that scales.
- Best practices for marketing your products on social media and increasing conversions.
- Automating your sales funnel with tools like Shopify, Kajabi, or BigCommerce.

Chapter 6

Becoming a Content Creator: Monetizing Your Passion

Content creation is rapidly becoming one of the most profitable careers of the future. In 2025, the content creation ecosystem will be more diversified and integrated with new platforms and monetization strategies.

Key Themes:

- **Monetizing Content:** From YouTube ads and Twitch streams to Patreon and Substack, content creators can earn money in multiple ways.

- **Short-Form Video & Streaming:** Why TikTok, Instagram Reels, and live-streaming on platforms like YouTube and Twitch are becoming major revenue sources.

- **Building a Loyal Audience:** The importance of community engagement, authenticity, and building a brand.

- **Diversified Revenue Streams:** Leveraging affiliate marketing, brand sponsorships, and merchandise sales to maximize income.

Actionable Advice:

- How to get started as a content creator, even with minimal followers.
- How to negotiate brand deals and partnerships that align with your audience.
- The benefits of creating multiple streams of revenue as a creator.

Chapter 7

Building a Future-Proof Career with AI and Automation

As AI and automation reshape many industries, individuals who learn to harness these technologies will be better positioned for success in the future. This chapter will discuss how you can future-proof your career by embracing AI, robotics, and other emerging technologies.

Key Themes:

- **AI-Enhanced Skills:** How AI can complement human work, including fields like customer service, programming, and healthcare.

- **Robotics and the Labor Market:** How automation will replace certain jobs but create new ones in fields like robotics maintenance, data science, and machine learning.

- **AI Entrepreneurship:** How to build and scale AI-driven businesses and startups.

- **Upskilling for the Future:** The importance of continuous learning, acquiring tech skills, and staying ahead of automation trends.

Actionable Advice:

- Resources for learning AI and automation technologies.
- How to use AI tools to enhance your productivity and creativity in any career.
- The best industries to focus on if you want to future-proof your career.

Chapter 8

The Importance of Networking and Building Relationships

In an increasingly digital and automated world, the value of human connections cannot be overstated. Networking will remain one of the most effective ways to open up new business opportunities and career paths.

Key Themes:

- Digital Networking: How to use platforms like LinkedIn, Twitter, and other social media to connect with industry leaders and potential collaborators.

- Creating Meaningful Relationships: The difference between transactional networking and building long-term, value-driven relationships.

- The Role of Mentorship: How finding a mentor or being a mentor can accelerate your career or business.

Actionable Advice:

- How to craft a strong LinkedIn profile and engage with professionals in your industry.
- Best practices for nurturing relationships through virtual events and social media.
- The power of collaboration and joint ventures in today's economy.

Shaping Your Financial Future in 2025 and Beyond

Digital Entrepreneurship & Online Businesses

Chapter 9

1. Start a YouTube Channel

Starting a YouTube channel and leveraging its algorithm to monetize your content can be an exciting and rewarding journey. Here's a step-by-step guide to help you get started, grow your audience, and turn your channel into a source of income through ads, sponsorships, and merchandise.

Step 1: Set Up Your YouTube Channel
Before you start creating content, you need to establish a solid foundation for your channel:

- **Create a Google Account:** If you don't already have one, sign up for a Google account, which will give you access to YouTube.

- **Create Your YouTube Channel:** Go to YouTube, sign in, and create your channel. Customize your profile picture, channel banner, and about section to make your channel visually appealing and informative.

- **Choose a Niche:** It's crucial to define your niche early. Focus on a specific topic you are passionate about, whether it's gaming, cooking, education, tech reviews, or vlogging. A niche helps attract a dedicated audience.

- **Branding:** Invest time in creating a memorable brand. This includes designing a logo, choosing channel colors, and establishing a consistent look across your videos. Consistent branding helps with recognition and viewer retention.

Step 2: Optimize Your Content for YouTube's Algorithm

YouTube's algorithm favors content that engages viewers and encourages them to watch for longer periods. Here's how to optimize your videos for the best performance:

- **Video Title:** Make sure your video titles are clear, engaging, and include relevant keywords. This will help your videos show up in search results and recommendations. For example, instead of "How to Bake a Cake," try "How to Bake a Perfect Chocolate Cake (Easy Recipe)."

- **Thumbnails:** Create eye-catching thumbnails that make viewers want to click on your video. Thumbnails should be high-quality and visually compelling. You can use tools like Canva or Photoshop to create them.

- **Description & Tags:** Write detailed video descriptions that explain what the video is about and include relevant keywords. Use tags to further help YouTube understand what your video is about, so it can recommend it to the right audience.

- **Engagement:** Encourage viewers to like, comment, and subscribe. The more engagement a video gets, the more likely YouTube will recommend it to others. Engage with your audience by responding to comments, asking questions, and creating content that encourages interaction.

- **Consistency:** Upload videos consistently, whether it's once a week, bi-weekly, or even daily. YouTube values channels that regularly produce content, and consistency helps build an audience over time.

Step 3: Grow Your Audience
Growing your channel requires time and effort, but with the right strategy, you can attract a loyal audience:

- **Collaborations:** Collaborating with other YouTubers in your niche can introduce your channel to new audiences. It's a win-win for both creators.

- **Cross-Promote on Social Media:** Share your videos on platforms like Instagram, Twitter, Facebook, and TikTok. This can drive traffic to your YouTube channel and help you build a broader following.

- **Content Variety:** Mix up your content format to keep things fresh. Try tutorials, challenges, Q&A sessions, behind-the-scenes videos, and live streams to appeal to different types of viewers.

- **SEO (Search Engine Optimization):** Research popular keywords and trends in your niche using tools like TubeBuddy or VidIQ. Incorporating these keywords into your video titles, descriptions, and tags will improve the discoverability of your content.

Step 4: Monetize Your YouTube Channel
Once you've built an audience and are getting regular views, you can start monetizing your channel through various revenue streams:

1. Ads (YouTube Partner Program)

To monetize your content through ads, you must first join the YouTube Partner Program (YPP). To qualify, you need:
- 1,000 subscribers
- 4,000 hours of watch time in the past 12 months
- A linked AdSense account

Once you're part of YPP, YouTube will place ads on your videos, and you'll earn money based on the number of views and clicks those ads receive.

Ad Revenue Tips:
- Focus on creating high-quality, engaging videos that keep viewers watching.
- Longer videos (over 10 minutes) tend to get more ad breaks, which can increase ad revenue.
- Videos with higher watch times and engagement often earn more.

2. Sponsorships

As your channel grows and attracts a substantial following, brands may approach you for sponsorships. Sponsorships involve promoting a product or service in exchange for payment.

- **How to Get Sponsorships:** Reach out to companies in your niche that align with your brand, or use influencer platforms (like GrapeVine, Channel Pages, or Famebit) to find sponsorship opportunities.

- **Create a Media Kit:** A media kit includes details about your audience demographics, engagement rates, and content performance. It helps potential sponsors see the value of working with you.

- **Be Authentic:** Only work with brands that align with your audience's interests. Authenticity is key to maintaining trust with your viewers.

3. Merchandise

Selling merchandise is a great way to monetize your brand, especially once you have a loyal fanbase. Platforms like Teespring, Spreadshirt, and Merch by Amazon integrate with YouTube, allowing you to promote and sell branded products directly to your viewers.

- **Create Merchandise:** Design custom T-shirts, hats, mugs, or phone cases with your logo or popular catchphrases from your videos.

- **Promote Merchandise in Your Videos:** Mention your merchandise in videos, add links in the description, and feature the products in your content.

- **Create Limited Edition Items:** Consider creating exclusive or limited-time merchandise for special events or milestones to drive urgency and sales.

Step 5: Analyze Performance and Adjust

To maximize revenue, you need to regularly monitor your channel's performance and adjust your strategy as needed.

- **YouTube Analytics:** Dive into your YouTube analytics to understand your audience demographics, watch time, traffic sources, and engagement metrics. This data will help you optimize your content for higher performance.

- **Experiment with Content:** Don't be afraid to try new formats, titles, or topics. See what resonates with your audience and adjust accordingly.

- **Audience Feedback:** Pay attention to comments and feedback from your audience. Use their insights to create content they want to see and improve the viewer experience.

Final Thoughts

Starting a YouTube channel and monetizing it through ads, sponsorships, and merchandise requires dedication, strategy, and consistency. By creating quality content, optimizing for YouTube's algorithm, engaging with your audience, and exploring multiple revenue streams, you can turn your passion into a sustainable business. Remember, success on YouTube doesn't happen overnight, so be patient, stay consistent, and always look for ways to improve and grow your channel.

Create an Online Course

Starting a business by creating and selling an online course is a fantastic way to share your knowledge, help others, and generate income. With platforms like Udemy, Teachable, and Skillshare, it's easier than ever to launch a course and reach a global audience. Here's a step-by-step guide to help you get started:

1. Identify Your Niche

The first step in creating a successful online course is identifying a niche that aligns with your expertise and passion. This could be anything from coding, marketing, cooking, photography, or even personal development. It's important to choose a subject that you are passionate about, as this enthusiasm will shine through in your teaching.

Key Considerations:

- What skills or knowledge do you have that others might want to learn?
- Is there demand for this topic? (Check forums, social media groups, and keyword tools to gauge interest.)
- Is the topic specific enough to stand out but broad enough to attract a large audience?

2. Research Your Target Audience

Understanding who you're creating your course for is crucial. Are you targeting beginners, intermediates, or advanced learners? What are their goals, pain points, and learning styles? Researching your audience will help you create content that speaks to their needs and learning preferences.

Methods to Understand Your Audience:

- Look at similar courses on platforms like Udemy, Coursera, or Teachable to see what topics are popular and read student reviews.
- Join relevant online communities (e.g., forums, Facebook groups, LinkedIn) to engage with potential learners.
- Use surveys or polls to ask your network what they would like to learn.

3. Choose the Right Platform

There are several platforms available to host and sell your online course, each with its pros and cons. Two popular choices are **Udemy** and **Teachable**:

  - **Udemy:** Udemy has a built-in audience and handles marketing, which can be helpful if you're just starting out. However, Udemy takes a percentage of your sales, and you have less control over pricing.

  - **Teachable:** Teachable allows you more control over pricing, branding, and marketing. You can set up a customized sales page and offer different pricing tiers. However, you're responsible for driving traffic and marketing your course.

Other Platforms to Consider:

  - **Skillshare:** A subscription-based model where you earn based on the number of minutes watched.

  - **Kajabi:** Great for building and scaling an entire course business with features like email marketing, landing pages, and advanced analytics.

  - **Thinkific:** Another good platform for creating and selling courses, offering flexible pricing plans and a range of customization options.

4. Create High-Quality Content

The heart of your online course is the content. The more engaging, clear, and practical your course is, the more likely students will complete it and leave positive reviews. Start by breaking your course down into manageable modules and lessons. Think about how you can deliver your content in an engaging way using video, quizzes, assignments, and downloadable resources.

Tips for Creating Great Content:

  - **Structure your course:** Outline your course into clear modules or lessons that follow a logical progression. Start with the basics and move toward more advanced topics.

  - **Engage with multimedia:** Use a mix of video, text, slides, and audio to keep things interesting. Many students prefer video-based content, so consider using screen recording software or a simple webcam setup.

  - **Keep lessons concise:** Avoid overwhelming learners with lengthy lectures. Aim for 5-10 minute videos to maintain attention.

- **Include quizzes and exercises:** Help students reinforce what they've learned through quizzes, challenges, and practical exercises.

5. Edit and Polish Your Course

Once you've created your course materials, take the time to edit and refine them. Good production quality matters, so ensure your videos are clear, well-lit, and have good sound. If needed, consider investing in a basic microphone or lighting equipment to improve the quality.

Things to Check:

- Video and audio clarity
- Professional-looking slides and visuals
- Accurate and error-free content
- Clear instructions and calls to action for students

6. Set Your Pricing Strategy

Deciding how to price your course is an important step. Pricing can vary depending on the length and depth of the course, as well as your target audience. You can offer discounts or bundles to incentivize people to purchase.

Pricing Strategies:

- **Competitive pricing:** Research similar courses to see what others are charging. Aim for competitive but fair pricing.

- **Tiered pricing:** Offer different price points for different levels of content. For example, a basic version of the course might be cheaper, and a premium version with additional support could be higher.

- **Discounts and promotions:** Platforms like Udemy allow for frequent promotions and sales. You can also create coupon codes to offer limited-time discounts.

  Free vs. Paid: While you can offer some courses for free, charging for your course gives you more control over its perceived value. Offering a free teaser lesson can help draw in potential customers.

7. Market Your Course

Marketing is key to selling your course. Once your course is ready, you need to drive traffic to it. Here are some strategies:

- **Social Media:** Leverage platforms like Instagram, Twitter, LinkedIn, and Facebook to promote your course. Share valuable content related to your course topic to build trust and generate interest.

- **Email Marketing:** Build an email list by offering free resources or a mini-course in exchange for email addresses. Once you've established a relationship, promote your course to your subscribers.

- **Affiliate Marketing:** Partner with influencers or bloggers in your niche who can help promote your course to their audience in exchange for a commission on sales.

- **Paid Advertising:** Use Facebook Ads, Google Ads, or even YouTube ads to drive targeted traffic to your course.

8. Launch Your Course

Once everything is in place, it's time for the launch! Create a buzz around your course before the official release. You can do this by offering early bird discounts, a limited-time bonus, or even hosting a webinar to introduce potential students to the content.

Launch Tips:

- **Pre-launch:** Build anticipation by teasing your course on social media and offering sneak peeks.

- **Launch day:** Have a special promotion or bonus available to encourage early sign-ups.

- **Post-launch:** Continue marketing your course with testimonials, success stories, and regular updates.

9. Engage with Your Students

After launching, the relationship with your students shouldn't end. Engage with them through discussion boards, live Q&A sessions, and email. Positive interactions will lead to great reviews, which can help your course gain traction. Encourage students to leave feedback and use it to improve future courses.

Ways to Engage:
- Respond to student questions promptly.

- Offer additional resources or bonus content for students who complete the course.
- Create a community (e.g., a private Facebook group or Slack channel) where students can share their progress.

10. Scale Your Business

Once your course is up and running, look for ways to scale. You can create additional courses in the same niche or expand to new topics. You might also consider offering one-on-one coaching or consulting services as an upsell.

Scaling Tips:

- **Expand your course catalog:** Offer more advanced courses or related topics.

- **Create a membership site:** Build a subscription-based model with ongoing learning resources and a community.

- **Automate marketing:** Use email marketing automation, content marketing, and retargeting ads to drive consistent sales.

Final Thoughts

Creating an online course can be a rewarding business venture, combining your expertise with the flexibility of online education. By choosing the right platform, developing high-quality content, and engaging with your audience, you can create a thriving online course business that allows you to earn income while helping others learn. Start small, stay consistent, and continue refining your approach as you grow!

Chapter 11

Launch an E-commerce Store

How to Launch an E-Commerce Store: Selling Physical Products or Dropshipping via Shopify or Etsy

Starting an e-commerce store has become increasingly accessible with platforms like Shopify and Etsy, which allow anyone to sell products online, whether they are physical goods or drop shipped items. Here's a step-by-step guide on how to launch your own e-commerce store using these popular platforms:

1. Define Your Niche and Business Model

Before diving into setting up your store, it's crucial to decide on the type of products you want to sell and the model you'll follow. Two popular business models in e-commerce are:

- **Selling Physical Products:** You purchase inventory upfront, store it, and handle the shipping yourself or via third-party logistics (3PL). This model gives you more control over product quality and customer experience.

- **Dropshipping:** You partner with suppliers who ship products directly to your customers. You don't need to handle inventory or shipping, but your margins can be smaller, and you have less control over product quality and fulfillment times.

Choosing a Niche

A profitable e-commerce store usually thrives in a specific niche. Whether it's custom jewelry, organic skincare, home decor, or tech gadgets, defining your niche helps to target a specific audience and stand out in a crowded market.

2. Choose Your Platform: Shopify or Etsy

Once you've settled on your business model, you need to select the platform that suits your needs best. Here's a breakdown of **Shopify** vs **Etsy**:

Shopify

- **Best for:** Entrepreneurs looking to scale a fully branded e-commerce store with a custom domain, a variety of payment methods, and integrations with third-party tools.

- **Features:** Shopify is a powerful e-commerce platform that allows you to create a fully customized online store. It offers tools for inventory management, payment gateways, shipping options, marketing integrations, and more.
- **Costs:** Shopify charges a monthly subscription fee (starting at $39/month), plus transaction fees.

- **Pros:** Full control over branding, marketing, and customer experience. Great for building a long-term, scalable business.

Etsy

- **Best for:** Creatives and small businesses that want to sell unique handmade, vintage, or craft products.

- **Features:** Etsy is a marketplace where you can list products and connect with buyers. It provides built-in traffic, but you're competing with other sellers on the platform.

- **Costs:** Etsy charges a listing fee ($0.20 per item) and takes a transaction fee (5% of the sale price) and a payment processing fee (varies by country).
- **Pros:** Etsy has an established audience looking for handmade, vintage, and unique products, which can make it easier to gain visibility without heavy marketing.

3. Set Up Your E-Commerce Store

For Shopify:

1. Sign up for an Account: Visit Shopify.com, and create an account. You'll need to provide basic details like your store name, email, and password.

2. Choose a Theme: Shopify offers both free and paid themes. Choose one that reflects your brand identity and suits the products you sell.

3. Add Products: For physical products, add detailed descriptions, high-quality images, and pricing. If you're dropshipping, you can use apps like Oberlo or Spocket to import products from suppliers directly.

4. Set Up Payment Gateways: Shopify supports various payment gateways, including credit cards, PayPal, and Shopify Payments.

5. Configure Shipping: Set up your shipping rates (flat rate, free shipping, or variable rates) based on your business model.

6. Customize Your Store: Add your logo, adjust the colors and fonts, and include essential pages like "About Us," "Contact," "Terms & Conditions," and "Return Policy."

7. Launch Your Store: After customizing, double-check everything, and once you're satisfied, launch your store. You can now start promoting it and driving traffic.

For Etsy:

1. Create an Etsy Account: Go to Etsy.com and sign up. Afterward, click on "Sell on Etsy" to set up your shop.

2. Choose Your Shop Name: Pick a unique and memorable name for your Etsy store. Etsy requires that the name be between 4-20 characters.

3. Add Listings: Upload product photos, write descriptions, set prices, and choose the category that best fits your products. Etsy allows you to set your shipping rates, as well.

4. Set Up Payment Options: Etsy allows you to accept payments via Etsy Payments, which includes credit cards, debit cards, and PayPal.

5. Customize Your Shop: Etsy allows some customization of your store's design, such as uploading a banner, shop icon, and crafting an "About" section to tell your story.

6. Launch Your Shop: Once your listings are live, your Etsy store will be visible to shoppers searching for products in your niche.

4. Market Your E-Commerce Store

Now that your store is set up, it's time to drive traffic and sales. Here are some marketing strategies:

- **Social Media Marketing:** Leverage platforms like Instagram, Facebook, Pinterest, and TikTok to promote your products. Share high-quality images, customer testimonials, and behind-the-scenes content to engage potential buyers.

- **Search Engine Optimization (SEO):** Optimize your product descriptions and images for SEO to appear in search engine results. Use keywords relevant to your products and niche.

- **Email Marketing:** Build an email list by offering discounts, newsletters, or content that adds value. Send regular updates and promotional offers to your subscribers.

- **Influencer Marketing:** Collaborate with influencers or bloggers in your niche to reach a broader audience and gain credibility.

- **Paid Ads:** Run targeted ads on platforms like Facebook, Instagram, or Google to drive traffic to your store.

5. Manage Your Orders and Customer Service

Once orders start coming in, it's important to efficiently manage fulfillment and provide excellent customer service.

- **Order Fulfillment:** If you're selling physical products, ensure you have a streamlined system for packing and shipping. For dropshipping, stay in touch with your suppliers to ensure timely delivery.

- **Customer Service:** Provide excellent support by responding to inquiries quickly and professionally. Address any concerns promptly to build customer loyalty.

6. Monitor Your Analytics and Improve
After your store is up and running, regularly check your sales data and website traffic. Platforms like Shopify have built-in analytics tools to track key metrics like:
- Traffic sources
- Conversion rates
- Average order value
- Abandoned carts

Use this data to optimize your product listings, marketing campaigns, and overall store performance. Constantly look for ways to improve and refine your processes.

Final Thoughts

Launching an e-commerce store—whether selling physical products or dropshipping—is an exciting journey that involves careful planning and execution. Shopify and Etsy are both excellent platforms, each offering unique advantages based on your needs. By choosing the right platform, curating a unique product offering, and effectively marketing your store, you can build a profitable e-commerce business that stands out in the digital marketplace.

Chapter 12

How to Develop a Mobile App: A Step-by-Step Guide

With mobile app usage soaring, the opportunity to create a successful app has never been greater. The global app economy is booming, and with the right idea and execution, building an app can be highly profitable. Whether you're focusing on fitness, productivity, entertainment, or another niche, the process of app development involves several key stages that can make or break your project's success.

1. Idea Validation and Market Research

Before diving into the development process, it's crucial to validate your app idea. This ensures there's demand for your product and that you're solving a real problem. Here's how to start:

- **Identify Your Target Audience:** Understand who your app will serve. Is it fitness enthusiasts, busy professionals, or gamers? Knowing your audience helps you design the app around their needs and preferences.

- **Market Research:** Analyze competitors in the niche you're targeting (fitness apps like MyFitnessPal, productivity apps like Todoist, or entertainment apps like Netflix). Identify their strengths, weaknesses, and the opportunities for differentiation.

- **User Surveys and Feedback:** Talk to potential users and gather insights about their pain points. This helps you refine your app's core features and functionality.

2. Define Your App's Features and Functionality

A well-defined set of features is the backbone of any successful app. When thinking about your app's functionality, consider:

- **Core Features:** What are the must-have features that make your app unique and valuable? For example, in a fitness app, this might include workout plans, progress tracking, and social sharing capabilities.

- **MVP (Minimum Viable Product):** Start with a basic version of your app with only the essential features. This allows you to launch quickly, gather feedback, and make improvements over time.

- **User Experience (UX) Design:** Focus on creating an intuitive and engaging experience. An app with poor UX design can cause users to abandon it quickly.

3. Choose the Right Technology Stack

Selecting the right technology stack is crucial for the performance and scalability of your app. You'll need to decide whether to develop for iOS, Android, or both platforms. Consider the following:

- **Native vs. Cross-Platform Development:** Native apps are built for a specific platform (iOS or Android) using the platform's native language, like Swift for iOS or Kotlin for Android. Cross-platform frameworks like React Native or Flutter allow you to write one codebase that works on both platforms.

- **Backend Infrastructure:** Choose the right backend technologies (e.g., Node.js, Ruby on Rails, or Django) to handle your app's data, user authentication, and other server-side logic.

- **Cloud Services:** Services like AWS, Google Cloud, or Firebase offer robust solutions for hosting, databases, and real-time features.

4. Design the User Interface (UI)

Design is critical to attracting and retaining users. The UI design should be simple, functional, and aligned with your brand identity. Focus on:

- **Consistent Branding:** Use colors, fonts, and logos that reflect your brand. Consistency in design builds trust and recognition.

- **Simplicity and Clean Layouts:** Ensure that the app is easy to navigate with clearly defined sections. A cluttered UI can confuse users and drive them away.

- **Responsive Design:** Make sure your app looks and functions well on different screen sizes and orientations (especially for tablets and smartphones).

5. App Development

Once you've got your features and design ready, it's time to start the development process. You can either hire a development team or work with a mobile app development agency. The app development process typically includes:

- **Front-End Development:** This is what users interact with. The front-end development focuses on implementing the UI design, handling user input, and integrating it with the backend.

- **Back-End Development:** This includes setting up databases, servers, and APIs that support the app's functionality. Back-end developers ensure that the app can scale as your user base grows.

- **Integration with Third-Party Services:** Many apps use third-party services for payment processing (like Stripe), location-based services (Google Maps), or social sharing. Make sure to integrate them smoothly.

6. Testing and Quality Assurance

Testing is a vital part of the app development process. You should conduct a variety of tests to ensure your app works as expected:

- **Functionality Testing:** Ensure all app features work correctly.

- **Usability Testing:** Test the user experience to make sure it's intuitive.

- **Performance Testing:** Check that the app runs smoothly, loads quickly, and can handle multiple users.

- **Device Testing**: Test your app on multiple devices and screen sizes to ensure compatibility. Bug-free, smooth performance is key to creating a positive user experience and keeping users engaged.

7. Launch Your App

Launching an app requires more than just pressing a button. A successful launch involves marketing and promotion strategies to get the word out. Here's how you can do it:

- **Pre-Launch Marketing:** Build excitement before launch through social media, email campaigns, and a landing page to capture early users.

- **App Store Optimization (ASO):** Optimize your app's listing in the App Store or Google Play Store with a compelling title, description, and relevant keywords.

- **Gather Reviews and Feedback:** Encourage early users to leave reviews and provide feedback so you can make improvements in future updates.

8. Post-Launch Monitoring and Updates

Once your app is live, the work doesn't stop there. You need to monitor performance and user engagement:

- **Analytics:** Use tools like Google Analytics for Firebase or Mixpanel to track how users are interacting with your app.

- **Bug Fixes and Updates:** Address bugs, improve functionality, and add new features based on user feedback. Regular updates are critical for maintaining a loyal user base.

- **Marketing and Retention:** Continuously market your app through ads, partnerships, and promotions. Use push notifications, email campaigns, and in-app messages to retain users.

9. Monetization Strategies

If you're aiming for profitability, you'll need a solid monetization strategy. Some common models include:

- **Freemium Model:** Offer a free version of the app with limited features and charge for premium features or content (e.g., in a fitness app, this could include access to advanced workout plans).

- **In-App Purchases:** Allow users to buy virtual goods, extra features, or subscriptions within the app (common in entertainment and gaming apps).

- **Ad Revenue:** Show ads in the app and earn money through ad impressions or clicks.

- **Subscription Model:** Offer recurring access to content or features, such as a monthly or yearly subscription to exclusive content or services.

10. Scaling and Improving

As your user base grows, you'll need to scale your infrastructure to handle increased traffic and usage. Additionally, continually gather user feedback to evolve your app, adding new features or improving existing ones to keep users engaged and satisfied.

Final Thoughts

Developing a successful mobile app in niches like fitness, productivity, or entertainment can be incredibly rewarding, but it requires careful planning and execution. From validating your idea and designing a seamless user experience to selecting the right technology stack and marketing your app effectively, each step plays a crucial role in the overall success of the project.
By staying focused on solving real problems for your target audience, ensuring top-notch quality, and iterating based on user feedback, you can create an app that not only attracts users but also becomes a profitable, long-term venture.

Chapter 13

How to Sell NFTs (Non-Fungible Tokens): A Step-by-Step Guide

Non-Fungible Tokens (NFTs) have revolutionized the way we think about ownership and value in the digital world. By creating and selling NFTs, you can turn your digital art, music, or virtual assets into verifiable, tradable assets on the blockchain. If you're an artist, musician, game designer, or anyone creating digital content, selling NFTs can offer a new and lucrative way to monetize your work. Here's a step-by-step guide to help you get started:

1. Create Your Digital Content

The first step is creating the digital asset that you want to sell as an NFT. This could be:

- **Digital Art:** Illustrations, paintings, graphic designs, animations, or other digital visual art forms.

- **Music & Audio Files:** Original songs, beats, soundscapes, or albums.

- **Virtual Assets or Collectibles:** These could be virtual items like skins, avatars, or in-game assets, such as a rare sword in a game or a virtual pet.
Ensure that the content is unique, as NFTs are valued for their scarcity and originality. High-quality work can attract more buyers.

2. Choose an NFT Marketplace

To sell your NFTs, you need to list them on an NFT marketplace. One of the most popular platforms is **OpenSea**, but there are other marketplaces that may suit different needs or types of content. Some of the top marketplaces include:
- **OpenSea:** One of the largest NFT platforms for all types of digital assets (art, music, collectibles, etc.).
- **Rarible:** A decentralized NFT marketplace that allows you to create and sell NFTs with ease.
- **Mintable:** A user-friendly platform to mint (create) and sell NFTs, which also offers an option for no upfront costs.
- **Foundation:** Known for high-quality art sales and artist-friendly features.
- **SuperRare:** A curated marketplace for artists to showcase and sell their digital art.
Each platform has its unique features and audience, so research and select one that fits your content best.

3. Set Up a Digital Wallet

NFTs are built on blockchain technology, typically on the Ethereum blockchain, although other blockchains like Solana or Tezos are also gaining popularity. To sell NFTs, you'll need a digital wallet that supports cryptocurrency and NFTs.
Some popular wallet options are:

- **MetaMask:** A browser extension that allows you to interact with Ethereum-based apps and manage your crypto assets.

- **Coinbase Wallet:** A wallet tied to your Coinbase account, making it easy to transfer crypto.

- **Trust Wallet:** A mobile-friendly wallet for managing NFTs and cryptocurrencies.
Make sure your wallet is properly connected to the NFT marketplace to facilitate the sale of your NFTs.

4. Mint Your NFT

"**Minting**" is the process of turning your digital asset into an NFT. When you mint an NFT, you create a unique token on the blockchain that represents ownership of your digital content. Most NFT platforms offer a simple process to mint your NFTs:

- **Upload Your Content:** On the marketplace, you'll be prompted to upload your digital art, music, or virtual assets.

- **Add Details:** You'll need to provide a name, description, and any additional details about the NFT, like the rarity or uniqueness of the item.

- **Set Royalties:** One of the advantages of NFTs is the ability to set royalty percentages. This means that every time your NFT is resold, you earn a commission, typically ranging from 5-10%. This creates a passive income stream for creators.

- **Mint the NFT:** Once your details are set, mint the NFT by confirming the transaction in your wallet. This will incur a small fee (known as a "**gas fee**") for the blockchain transaction.

5. Set Your Price

Deciding on the right price for your NFT can be challenging. Here are some tips:

- **Fixed Price:** You set a specific price for your NFT. Once someone buys it, the transaction is complete.

- **Auction:** You can set up an auction, where potential buyers place bids over a specified period. At the end of the auction, the highest bid wins the NFT.

- **Edition Size:** If you want to create a limited series of your work, you can set the number of copies available for sale. Limited editions can drive demand and increase the value of the NFTs.

6. Promote Your NFT

Once your NFT is listed, promotion is key to driving attention and sales. Here are a few strategies:

- **Social Media:** Share your NFT on platforms like Twitter, Instagram, and TikTok. Use relevant hashtags like #NFTArt, #CryptoArt, #NFTCommunity, etc. to reach a larger audience.

- **Discord:** Many NFT communities operate through Discord, where you can engage with other creators and collectors.

- **Collaborate with Influencers:** Reach out to influencers or NFT enthusiasts who can help promote your work.

- **Create a Website:** A personal website with a portfolio and links to your NFT listings can give buyers more confidence in your work.

- **Engage with the Community:** Build relationships with potential buyers and other artists in the NFT space. Participate in online forums, Discord groups, or Twitter Spaces.

7. Sell Your NFT

When someone buys your NFT, the transaction is processed on the blockchain, and the buyer's wallet will be credited with the NFT. As the seller, you will receive payment in the form of cryptocurrency (usually Ethereum, depending on the marketplace).

- **Gas Fees:** Be aware of transaction fees, especially when minting or transferring NFTs on platforms like Ethereum. Gas fees can fluctuate based on network congestion.

- **Royalties:** As mentioned earlier, you can set royalties, meaning you'll earn a percentage of sales every time the NFT is resold.

8. Keep Track of Your Earnings and Taxes

After successfully selling your NFT, keep track of your earnings, especially if you plan to sell multiple pieces. In many countries, income generated from NFTs is taxable, so it's important to maintain accurate records and consult a tax professional.

Final Thoughts

Selling NFTs can be a rewarding way to monetize your digital creations, but it requires time, effort, and understanding of the digital asset market. By following these steps and engaging with the vibrant NFT community, you can unlock new opportunities to showcase your work and generate income. Be creative, stay informed, and enjoy the exciting world of NFTs!

Chapter 14

Affiliate Marketing

Affiliate marketing is a popular way to earn income online by promoting products or services from brands or companies, and earning a commission on each sale or action that results from your promotion. It's a performance-based business model that rewards you for driving customers to a company's website or landing page. Here's a step-by-step guide on how to get started with affiliate marketing:

1. Choose a Niche

To succeed in affiliate marketing, it's important to select a niche that you're passionate about or have expertise in. This could be anything from technology and fashion to health and fitness. A well-defined niche allows you to target a specific audience and become an authority in that area, which makes it easier to promote relevant products and services.

- **Tip:** Pick a niche with both high demand and enough affiliate programs to choose from.

2. Find Affiliate Programs

Once you have your niche, the next step is to find affiliate programs that match your content and audience. Many companies offer affiliate programs, and there are also affiliate networks that connect you with multiple brands at once.

- **Affiliate Networks:** These platforms host numerous affiliate programs from various companies. Examples include:
  - **Amazon Associates** (great for beginners)
  - **ShareASale**
  - **ClickBank**
  - **CJ Affiliate**
  - **Rakuten Marketing**
- **Direct Affiliate Programs:** Many companies offer their own affiliate programs, which you can join directly. This is common for larger companies or niche businesses that want to work with specific affiliates.

3. Sign Up for Affiliate Programs

Once you've found a few affiliate programs that suit your niche, you need to sign up for them. This usually involves creating an account and submitting some basic information about your website or platform. After approval, you'll get an affiliate link (or tracking link) that tracks sales or actions generated by your marketing efforts.

- **Tip:** Be selective about the affiliate programs you join. Make sure the products are relevant to your audience and that the commission structure is reasonable.

4. Create Quality Content

The key to successful affiliate marketing is creating valuable content that resonates with your audience. The better your content, the more likely your audience is to click on your affiliate links and make a purchase.
- Types of Content for Affiliate Marketing:
  - **Blog Posts and Articles:** Write detailed product reviews, comparisons, and tutorials.
  - **YouTube Videos:** Create video reviews, unboxings, or how-to guides.
  - **Social Media Posts:** Share tips, product recommendations, or influencer-style posts on Instagram, TikTok, or Twitter.
  - **Email Newsletters:** Send personalized offers or product recommendations directly to your subscribers.
  - **Podcasts:** Promote products in an organic, conversational way on your show.

- **Tip:** Focus on solving a problem or fulfilling a need for your audience. The more helpful and relevant your content is, the more likely people will trust your recommendations.

5. Integrate Affiliate Links Naturally

Rather than aggressively pushing products, integrate affiliate links naturally into your content. The goal is to make the promotions feel like valuable recommendations, not hard sells.

- Best Practices for Affiliate Link Placement:
  - Include affiliate links in your blog post where it makes sense contextually (e.g., in a product review or how-to guide).
  - Use call-to-action buttons or links that encourage readers to check out the product.
  - Ensure that your affiliate links don't interrupt the user experience. They should enhance the content, not distract from it.

- **Tip:** Disclose your affiliate relationships transparently with a disclaimer. For example, a statement like "This post contains affiliate links, meaning I may earn a small commission if you make a purchase through these links." This builds trust with your audience and complies with legal requirements (FTC guidelines).

6. Drive Traffic to Your Content

Without traffic, even the best affiliate content won't generate any sales. Driving traffic to your website or content is essential for affiliate marketing success. There are many ways to increase traffic to your platform, including:

- **Search Engine Optimization (SEO):** Optimize your content to rank higher in search engine results for relevant keywords.

- **Paid Advertising:** Use platforms like Google Ads or Facebook Ads to drive targeted traffic to your affiliate content.

- **Social Media Marketing:** Promote your content on social media platforms like Instagram, YouTube, Pinterest, or TikTok.

- **Email Marketing:** Build an email list and send targeted emails to your audience with affiliate offers and content.

- **Collaborations and Guest Posts:** Work with other influencers or bloggers in your niche to share your affiliate links with their audiences.

7. Monitor Your Results

As you promote affiliate products, it's important to track your performance. Most affiliate programs provide tracking dashboards where you can see how many clicks, conversions, and sales you've generated.
- **Key Metrics to Monitor:**
  - **Click-Through Rate (CTR):** How many people click your affiliate links compared to how many saw them.
  - **Conversion Rate:** How many clicks result in actual purchases or sign-ups.
  - **Earnings Per Click (EPC):** The average amount of money you earn for every click on your affiliate link.
  - **Total Earnings:** How much commission you've earned over a given period.

Monitoring these metrics will help you understand which products and marketing strategies are working best, and where you might need to improve.

8. Scale Your Affiliate Marketing Efforts

Once you've learned what works, you can scale up your efforts to increase your income. Here are a few ways to do this:

- **Create More Content:** Increase the volume of high-quality content to target more keywords and audiences.

- **Expand to Other Platforms:** If you've been focusing on one platform (like your blog), consider expanding to YouTube, TikTok, or email marketing.

- **Diversify Affiliate Programs:** Join additional affiliate programs or promote a variety of products to diversify your income streams.

- **Leverage Automation:** Use tools like email marketing automation or content scheduling tools to streamline your workflow.

9. Stay Ethical and Transparent

Successful affiliate marketers build long-term relationships with their audiences based on trust. Always prioritize providing value over making a sale. Promote products that you genuinely believe in, and avoid recommending things just for the sake of earning a commission.
By staying authentic and offering real value to your audience, you can build a sustainable and profitable affiliate marketing business.

Final Thoughts

Affiliate marketing is a great way to earn passive income by promoting products or services from companies and earning commissions on sales. Success in affiliate marketing requires choosing a niche, finding relevant affiliate programs, creating high-quality content, driving traffic to your content, and tracking your results. With patience, consistency, and dedication, you can build a profitable affiliate marketing business.

Chapter 15

Virtual Consulting or Coaching

How to Offer Virtual Consulting or Coaching Services

In today's digital age, offering virtual consulting or coaching has become an excellent way to monetize your expertise and connect with clients globally. Whether you're a business consultant, life coach, fitness expert, or specialist in any niche, providing one-on-one sessions remotely can be a rewarding and flexible way to share your knowledge. Here's how you can get started:

1. Identify Your Niche and Expertise

- **Find Your Area of Expertise:** Before you begin offering virtual consulting or coaching, define your niche. What are you particularly skilled at? It could be anything from career coaching, digital marketing consulting, financial advising, personal development, to fitness training or even niche hobbies. The more specific your niche, the more likely you'll attract clients who are looking for specialized help.

- **Assess Your Target Audience:** Who can benefit from your expertise? Are they businesses, individuals, or specific groups like students or professionals? Understanding your target market will help you create focused services that meet their needs.

2. Choose the Right Platform to Offer Your Services

You have several options for offering virtual consulting or coaching sessions. Here are two main routes to consider:

- **Using a Third-Party Platform (e.g., Clarity.fm)**

Platforms like **Clarity.fm**, **Coach.me**, or **Superpeer** are ideal for consultants and coaches who want to reach clients without needing to manage a website or deal with the technical side of scheduling and payments.

Steps to Get Started on Clarity.fm:

- **Create a Profile:** Sign up on the platform and set up a profile that highlights your expertise, background, and what you can offer. Be sure to include a professional photo, a compelling bio, and detailed information on the types of services you provide.

- **Set Your Rates:** Clarity.fm allows you to set an hourly rate for your sessions. Look at what other experts in your field are charging to get an idea of industry standards, and adjust accordingly based on your experience.

- **Market Your Services:** Promote your Clarity profile on social media, your email list, and through networking. A great way to get started is to offer free or discounted sessions to build reviews and credibility.

- **Be Available:** Respond to client requests quickly and manage your schedule effectively. Consistency and availability are key to building a loyal client base.

- Starting Your Own Website
If you prefer full control over your business, consider setting up your own website to offer consulting or coaching services. You can use website builders like **WordPress**, **Wix**, or **Squarespace** to create a professional-looking site.

Steps to Get Started with Your Own Website:

- **Domain and Hosting:** Choose a domain name that reflects your services and is easy to remember (e.g., www.YourExpertise.com). Purchase hosting through platforms like **Bluehost** or **SiteGround** to get your website online.

- **Create Service Pages:** Include detailed pages outlining the services you offer, pricing, testimonials, and FAQs. A booking system like **Acuity Scheduling** or **Calendly** can allow clients to schedule sessions with you directly.

- **Content Marketing:** Use blog posts, videos, podcasts, or webinars to showcase your expertise. Regular content creation helps attract organic traffic and build trust with potential clients.

- **Payment Integration:** Set up payment gateways like **PayPal**, **Stripe**, or use tools like **Square** to process payments. Having clear pricing and payment options makes it easy for clients to book and pay for their sessions.

- **Email List:** Building an email list is essential for nurturing relationships with potential clients. Offer free resources or eBooks in exchange for email subscriptions, and then use email marketing to stay in touch.

3. Promote Your Virtual Consulting or Coaching Business

Whether you use a platform like Clarity.fm or run your own site, promotion is key to growing your client base. Here are some strategies for gaining visibility:

- **Social Media:** Use platforms like LinkedIn, Instagram, Facebook, and X (formerly Twitter) to share valuable insights and advertise your consulting or coaching services. Posting testimonials, behind-the-scenes content, or client success stories can help build credibility.

- **Content Creation:** As a consultant or coach, your content is one of the best ways to demonstrate your expertise. Start a blog or create educational videos to attract a larger audience. Offering free resources like downloadable guides, worksheets, or email courses can entice people to book a session with you.

- **Networking:** Attend virtual events, webinars, and conferences relevant to your niche. Building relationships with other professionals in your industry can lead to collaborations and referrals.

- **Referral Programs:** Encourage past clients to refer others by offering incentives such as discounts or additional free sessions.

4. Optimize Your Consulting or Coaching Sessions

- **Set Clear Goals for Each Session:** Have a structured approach to each session, whether it's a coaching conversation or a business consultation. Be clear on the outcomes your client expects, and offer actionable advice.

- **Use Video Conferencing Tools:** Tools like **Zoom**, **Google Meet**, or **Skype** are great for conducting virtual sessions. Ensure you have a stable internet connection, proper lighting, and a quiet space to ensure a professional environment.

- **Provide Resources:** After each session, provide your clients with summaries, resources, or action plans to help them implement what they've learned.

- **Follow-Up:** Follow up with clients to track progress, provide ongoing support, and invite them to book additional sessions as needed.

5. Scale Your Virtual Consulting or Coaching Business

Once you've built a client base, you can scale your business in several ways:

- **Group Coaching:** Offer group sessions for clients who are interested in a more affordable option. Group coaching can be done through Zoom or other platforms and can expand your reach.

- **Create Online Courses:** If you find that certain topics come up repeatedly in your sessions, consider creating an online course or workshop. Platforms like **Teachable** or **Udemy** make it easy to package your expertise into digital products.

- **Hire Support:** As your business grows, consider hiring virtual assistants or other experts to help manage scheduling, marketing, or content creation.

6. Maintain Consistency and Quality

Consistency is key to sustaining a successful virtual consulting or coaching business. Continuously improve your skills, stay updated on trends in your niche, and keep honing your ability to provide valuable solutions to your clients.

By offering virtual consulting or coaching, you're able to share your expertise with a global audience, enjoy flexible working hours, and build a scalable business. Whether you use an established platform or run your own site, the possibilities are endless. The key is to stay committed, keep refining your offerings, and continue to deliver value to your clients.

Chapter 16

Create a Subscription Service or Membership Site

Creating a subscription service or membership site is a powerful way for creators to build a sustainable income stream while offering exclusive content to their audience. Platforms like **Patreon** and **Substack** have made it easier than ever for creators in fields like writing, music, art, and video to monetize their work through recurring subscriptions. Here's how you can create your own subscription service or membership site and leverage these platforms for success:

1. Define Your Niche and Value Proposition

Before you dive into setting up your subscription service, it's essential to understand your audience and what unique value you can offer them. Think about:

- **Your content:** What kind of content do you produce? (e.g., articles, videos, podcasts, art, music)

- **Your audience:** Who is most likely to benefit from and be willing to pay for your content? Are they niche hobbyists, business professionals, or general enthusiasts?

- **Exclusive offerings:** What will make your subscription worth the price? Will you offer behind-the-scenes content, early access, personal interactions, or members-only perks?

Tip: A clear, targeted niche makes your offerings more appealing, and people are more likely to subscribe if they feel they're getting something unique or valuable.

2. Choose the Right Platform

Selecting the right platform is crucial, as it will determine the ease of setup, how you manage subscribers, and how you interact with your community. Two of the most popular platforms are:

- **Patreon:** Great for creators in various fields (e.g., artists, writers, musicians, podcasters). It allows you to set up tiered subscription levels with different benefits, and it offers tools to communicate directly with your community, offer exclusive content, and manage memberships.

- **Substack:** Primarily focused on writers and newsletter creators, Substack allows you to publish and monetize newsletters with ease. Substack is more streamlined than Patreon, with a strong focus on content delivery and audience engagement.
Both platforms provide recurring revenue through subscriptions and can integrate with various tools (like email, social media, and payment processors).

3. Design Your Membership Tiers or Pricing Structure

Most successful membership sites use a tiered subscription model, where subscribers can choose from different levels of support with corresponding benefits. When designing your pricing structure, consider the following:

- **Low-cost options:** This encourages more people to subscribe. For example, you could have a $3-$5 per month tier that offers basic access to content, like exclusive blog posts or early access to videos.

- **Mid-level tiers:** At $10-$20 per month, you could offer additional perks like downloadable resources, exclusive webinars, or even direct interaction with you via Q&A sessions.

- **Premium tiers:** For your highest-paying members (e.g., $50+ per month), offer personalized content, one-on-one consultations, or early bird access to new releases.
It's important to balance accessibility with exclusivity. Offering a mix of price points allows you to engage with a wider audience while rewarding loyal supporters.

4. Create High-Quality, Exclusive Content

Your subscription service will only succeed if you're offering content that people can't easily find elsewhere. Some ideas for exclusive content include:

- **Behind-the-scenes access:** Share the process of creating your work or give a peek into your personal life.

- **Premium content:** Early access to articles, videos, or product releases.

- **Interactive content:** Live Q&As, member-only polls, or exclusive webinars.

- **Exclusive perks:** Digital downloads (e.g., eBooks, music tracks, templates), discounts on products, or personalized messages.
The key is to consistently offer something valuable and exclusive to your paying subscribers that they can't get from your free content.

5. Engage With Your Community

Building a community around your content is essential to long-term success. Engaged subscribers are more likely to continue their membership, promote your work, and contribute to your growth. Consider:

- **Regular communication:** Engage with your audience through newsletters, personal messages, or live events. Keeping in touch with your members builds a sense of belonging.

- **Exclusive social spaces:** Platforms like Discord or Slack allow creators to build private communities where members can interact with each other and the creator.

- **Rewards for loyal members:** Recognizing milestones, offering shoutouts, or giving members access to exclusive features is a great way to build loyalty.

6. Promote Your Subscription Service

Once you've set up your subscription site, it's time to get the word out. Promotion is critical for attracting subscribers:

- **Leverage social media:** Use platforms like Instagram, Twitter, and TikTok to give teasers about your content, share snippets, or invite followers to join your membership program.

- **Offer free content:** Offering free trials or free sample content can entice potential subscribers to join your paid tiers.

- **Collaborations and partnerships:** Work with other creators or influencers who have an audience that aligns with yours. This can help increase your visibility and bring in new members.

7. Monitor and Adjust

Once your subscription service is up and running, it's important to track key metrics such as:

- **Subscriber growth:** Are you attracting new members consistently? Are some tiers more popular than others?

- **Engagement levels:** How often are subscribers interacting with your content?

- **Retention rates:** Are your members sticking around, or are they dropping off after a month or two?
Based on this data, you can refine your offerings, adjust pricing, or modify your promotional strategies.

8. Consider Other Monetization Strategies

While subscriptions are a great primary revenue model, you can also integrate other income streams into your membership program, such as:

- **Affiliate marketing:** If you recommend products or services that align with your niche, affiliate links can generate additional revenue.

- **Sponsorships and partnerships:** As your membership grows, you might attract brands that want to sponsor your content or collaborate with you.

- **One-time product sales:** Offering physical products, digital downloads, or services to your community can provide an additional revenue stream.

Final Thoughts

Creating a subscription service or membership site is a powerful way for creators to build a recurring revenue stream while delivering consistent value to their audience. By choosing the right platform, offering valuable and exclusive content, engaging with your community, and promoting your site, you can build a thriving business around your creative work. Platforms like **Patreon** and **Substack** make it easier than ever to get started, but the key to success is a deep understanding of your audience, your niche, and the unique value you provide.

Chapter 17

How to Create a Subscription Service or Membership Site

1. Define Your Niche and Value Proposition

Before you start, identify the specific audience you want to target and what unique value you can offer them. Think about:
- **Who is your ideal subscriber?** (e.g., writers, artists, fitness enthusiasts, entrepreneurs)
- **What exclusive content or benefits will they receive?** (e.g., early access to content, behind-the-scenes looks, premium resources, Q&A sessions)
- **What makes your offering stand out from others?** (e.g., unique insights, personalized interactions, a specific theme or style)

2. Choose the Right Platform

Several platforms cater to subscription models, each offering a different set of features. The choice depends on the type of content you create and the level of customization you want.

- **Patreon:** Best for creators who want to offer exclusive content like videos, posts, tutorials, and live streams. It's a great choice for artists, musicians, writers, and podcasters.

- **Substack:** Ideal for writers and bloggers who want to send email newsletters and offer written content like articles, essays, or newsletters.

- **Memberful:** A more customizable platform that integrates with your website to offer memberships and subscriptions directly from your site.

- **Ko-fi:** A simpler and more accessible platform for creators, allowing for one-time donations as well as memberships. Perfect for hobbyists or creators with a smaller following.

- **Gumroad:** A versatile platform that allows creators to sell both digital and physical products and offer subscriptions for access to ongoing content.

3. Set Up Your Subscription Tiers

Offering different pricing tiers helps cater to a variety of budgets and incentivizes higher-level subscriptions. For example:

- **Basic Tier:** Access to basic content, such as blog posts, newsletters, or lower-quality videos.

- **Mid-Tier:** Includes exclusive content, bonus material, or early access to content.

- **Premium Tier:** Offers one-on-one interactions, personalized content, or exclusive live streams and workshops.

Pro Tip: Make sure each tier offers clear value relative to its price point, and ensure that each upgrade feels like a step up in terms of content or access.

4. Create Compelling Content

The key to a successful subscription service is delivering content that your audience will find valuable and engaging. Some ideas include:

- **Exclusive Videos:** Share tutorials, behind-the-scenes footage, or special performances.

- **Private Blogs or Newsletters:** Offer deeper insights, expert advice, or personal stories.

- **Online Communities:** Create private groups or forums where members can interact, discuss content, and connect.

- **Q&A Sessions or AMAs (Ask Me Anything):** Host live interactions where subscribers can ask you questions directly.

- **Exclusive Downloads or Resources:** Provide templates, guides, printables, or digital art as part of your membership.

5. Set Pricing and Payment Terms

- Decide whether you'll charge monthly, quarterly, or annually.
- Some creators offer discounted pricing for annual memberships to encourage long-term commitments.
- Platforms like Patreon and Substack handle payments automatically, but be transparent about pricing and any fees.

Example pricing strategy:

- **$5 per month:** Access to basic content and updates.
- **$10 per month:** Early access and behind-the-scenes content.
- **$25 per month:** Personalized advice, one-on-one calls, and VIP access to events.

6. Promote Your Membership Site

To build a successful subscription service, you need to effectively promote your offering to your target audience. Here are some strategies:

- **Leverage Social Media:** Use platforms like Instagram, Twitter, YouTube, and TikTok to promote your exclusive content and give sneak peeks of what subscribers can expect.
- **Collaborate with Influencers or Fellow Creators:** Partnering with others in your niche can help expand your reach.
- **Offer Free Previews:** Give potential subscribers a taste of your premium content through a free trial or teaser videos/articles.
- **Email Marketing:** If you already have a mailing list, use it to promote your new subscription offering with exclusive sign-up bonuses.
- **Create a Landing Page:** If you're using a platform like Memberful, you can create a custom landing page that clearly explains the benefits of joining your community.

7. Engage with Your Subscribers

Building a subscription service isn't just about content creation—it's also about community building. Stay engaged with your subscribers by:
- Responding to comments and messages regularly.
- Asking for feedback and incorporating it into future content.
- Hosting live chats or AMAs to connect directly with your audience.
- Offering rewards or bonuses for loyal subscribers (e.g., exclusive merchandise, shoutouts, or access to special events).

8. Track Your Metrics and Optimize

Once your subscription service is live, it's important to keep track of key metrics to ensure your success. Monitor:

- **Subscriber Growth:** Are you gaining new subscribers? Which tiers are most popular?

- **Engagement Rates:** Are people interacting with your content (e.g., liking, commenting, viewing)?

- **Churn Rate:** How many subscribers are you losing over time, and why?

Use this data to adjust your pricing, content, and promotional strategies. You may need to experiment with different types of content or promotional offers to see what resonates best with your audience.

9. Scale Your Subscription Service

As your audience grows, you may want to scale your business. Consider:
- Offering additional tiers with more exclusive content.
- Hiring help to manage community interactions, content creation, or administrative tasks.
- Creating a robust marketing plan to attract a broader audience.
- Exploring additional monetization options, like selling digital products or hosting paid workshops.

Final Thoughts

Starting a subscription service or membership site is a powerful way to generate recurring income and build a loyal community around your content. By offering unique, valuable content and engaging with your subscribers regularly, you can create a thriving business that scales over time.

Chapter 18

Start a Podcast

Step 1: Choose Your Niche and Define Your Audience

Before you hit record, think about the type of podcast you want to create. To build a loyal audience and attract sponsors, it's essential to focus on a specific niche. Consider:

- **Your passion and expertise:** What topics can you speak about with authority and enthusiasm?

- **Target audience:** Who will benefit most from your content? Are they fans of a specific hobby, industry, or subject?

A well-defined niche helps attract a dedicated audience, which is critical for both growing your podcast and monetizing it.

Step 2: Plan Your Podcast Content

- **Episode Format:** Will your podcast be interviews, storytelling, educational, or conversational? Decide on the structure.

- **Episode Frequency and Length:** How often will you release episodes? Will it be weekly, bi-weekly, or monthly? Also, determine how long each episode will be.

- **Outline Topics:** Create a list of episodes you'd like to produce in advance. This helps keep your content organized and consistent.

Step 3: Get the Right Equipment
Invest in the necessary equipment to produce high-quality audio:

- **Microphone:** A good quality microphone (e.g., Audio-Technica AT2020, Shure SM7B) is essential.

- **Headphones:** A reliable pair of closed-back headphones to monitor sound quality.

- **Recording and Editing Software:** Popular options include Audacity (free), Adobe Audition (paid), or GarageBand (for Mac users).

- **Hosting Platform:** Use podcast hosting services like Buzzsprout, Libsyn, or Anchor to upload your episodes. These platforms help distribute your podcast to directories like Spotify, Apple Podcasts, and Google Podcasts.

Step 4: Record and Edit Your Episodes

- **Recording:** Use your chosen software to record your episodes. Record in a quiet space to minimize background noise.

- **Editing:** Edit for clarity and conciseness, removing any unnecessary filler words, pauses, or mistakes. Use software like Audacity or GarageBand to clean up your audio.

- **Add Music & Branding:** Include intro and outro music (be sure to use royalty-free tracks) and consider creating a branded sound that reflects your podcast's personality.

Step 5: Publish and Promote

- **Upload Your Episodes:** Once you've recorded and edited your episodes, upload them to your hosting platform.

- **Submit to Directories:** Make sure your podcast is available on major podcast directories like Apple Podcasts, Spotify, Google Podcasts, and others.

- **Promotion:** Promote each episode on social media, your website, and through email newsletters. Engage with your listeners and encourage them to share your podcast.

Step 6: Monetize Your Podcast

Once you've built an audience and consistently produced content, you can start monetizing your podcast through several strategies:

1. Sponsorships and Advertisements

- **How it works:** Brands or companies may want to advertise on your podcast by paying for ad space. Ads are usually placed at the beginning, middle, or end of an episode.

- **Getting Sponsors:** Reach out to brands that align with your niche or audience. You can also sign up for podcast ad networks (e.g., Podcorn, AdvertiseCast) to connect with potential sponsors.

- **Audience Metrics:** Sponsors will likely want to know your audience size and engagement (downloads, listens, etc.). Use your podcast hosting platform's analytics to track these metrics and showcase them to potential sponsors.

2. Listener Donations and Crowdfunding

- **How it works:** Directly ask your audience for support in exchange for special content or perks.

- **Platforms for Donations:** Platforms like Patreon, Ko-fi, or Buy Me a Coffee allow your listeners to contribute financially in exchange for exclusive benefits like:
  - Behind-the-scenes content
  - Early access to episodes
  - Merchandise discounts
- **Incentives:** Provide value to your listeners by offering tiered donation levels, where supporters can access exclusive content, live Q&A sessions, or a shout-out on the show.

3. Premium Episodes or Subscriptions

  - **How it works:** Create exclusive content available only to paying subscribers.
  - **Options for Premium Content:**
  - **Bonus Episodes:** Offer bonus or extended episodes only for subscribers.
  - **Early Access:** Give paying listeners early access to new episodes before they go live to the public.
    - **Ad-Free Content:** Offer ad-free versions of your episodes to premium subscribers.
- **Platforms to Use:** Services like Patreon, Supercast, or Podbean support creating subscription models for premium content.

4. Affiliate Marketing

- **How it works:** Promote products or services relevant to your audience in exchange for a commission on sales made through your referral links.

- **Examples of Affiliate Programs:** Amazon Associates, ShareASale, or affiliate programs offered by companies in your niche.

- **How to Implement:** Mention affiliate products during your episodes and include links in the show notes or website. For best results, only promote products that align with your audience's interests.

5. Merchandise Sales

- How it works: Create branded merchandise (T-shirts, mugs, stickers) and sell them to your fans.

- Platforms to Use: Print-on-demand services like Teespring or Redbubble make it easy to design and sell merchandise without upfront costs. Simply upload your designs, and these services handle production and shipping.

6. Live Events or Virtual Meetups

- How it works: Once your podcast has a strong following, consider hosting live events, webinars, or virtual meetups where fans can interact with you directly. These can be ticketed events.

- In-person events: Host live podcasts or Q&A sessions at conventions or meetups, selling tickets for entry.

- Virtual Events: Hold exclusive virtual events for subscribers or a wider audience, using platforms like Zoom or YouTube Live.

Step 7: Measure and Optimize

- Track Performance: Use podcast analytics tools (e.g., from your hosting platform) to track key metrics like audience growth, episode downloads, listener demographics, and engagement.

- Iterate: Use feedback from your audience and performance data to refine your content, improve the listener experience, and optimize your monetization strategies.

Final Thoughts

Starting and monetizing a podcast is a long-term effort that requires dedication and strategy. Focus on creating high-quality content that resonates with your audience, and as your listener base grows, gradually implement monetization methods like sponsorships, donations, premium content, and affiliate marketing. Be patient, stay consistent, and always listen to your audience for ways to improve your podcast and revenue opportunities.
Remember to stay consistent, listen to your audience, and keep refining your offerings to meet their needs.
Starting a podcast and monetizing it effectively can be a rewarding venture, but it requires planning, consistency, and strategy.

Section 2. Tech-driven Opportunities

Chapter 19

AI & Chatbot Development

How to Develop AI & Chatbot Solutions for Customer Service Automation

Building AI-powered chatbots or virtual assistants can significantly improve customer service by automating common interactions, providing 24/7 support, and reducing the workload of human agents. Below is a step-by-step guide on how to develop and deploy effective AI-powered chatbots for businesses.

1. Define the Objective and Use Case

Before diving into the development process, it's crucial to clearly define the purpose of the chatbot and how it will assist in customer service. Consider the following questions:

- **What specific tasks should the chatbot perform?** (e.g., answering FAQs, processing orders, booking appointments, handling complaints)

- **What are the common customer queries?** (gather data from customer service logs or feedback)

- **How will the chatbot improve customer experience?** (e.g., reduce wait time, provide instant responses, handle repetitive questions)

2. Choose the Right AI Technology and Framework

There are several AI and machine learning technologies you can leverage to build an effective chatbot:

- **Natural Language Processing (NLP):** This is essential for understanding and processing human language. Popular NLP frameworks include:

  - **Dialogflow (by Google)**

  - **IBM Watson Assistant**

  - **Microsoft Azure Bot Services**

- Rasa (open-source)

- **Machine Learning Models:** These models are responsible for improving the chatbot's ability to understand context, intent, and entity recognition over time.

-**Pre-built Bot Development Platforms:** For those who want a no-code or low-code approach, platforms like **ManyChat**, **Tidio**, or **Chatfuel** may be useful.

3. Design the Conversational Flow

Map out how the chatbot will interact with users:

- **Intents:** Define user intentions (e.g., "ask about product availability," "check order status").

- **Entities:** These are the specific pieces of information the chatbot needs to extract (e.g., product names, order numbers, locations).

- **Dialog Flows:** Design step-by-step interactions and the possible variations of conversations based on user input. Tools like **Botmock** or **Lucidchart** can help in visually designing the flow.

- **Fallback Mechanisms:** Ensure the bot can handle unexpected queries by either asking for clarification or escalating to a human agent when necessary.

4. Develop the Chatbot

Once the objectives, AI models, and conversational design are in place, start building the chatbot:

- **Create Intent Recognition:** Set up the chatbot to recognize different types of user input (e.g., greetings, inquiries, or complaints) using NLP.

- **Build Response Logic:** Develop responses based on the identified intent. You can use predefined scripts or dynamic data fetched from external databases (e.g., order status or FAQs).

- **Integrate APIs and Databases:** For more advanced features, such as checking inventory or processing payments, integrate APIs that connect the chatbot to your business's systems.

5. Train the Chatbot

A successful AI chatbot learns from interactions to improve its performance:

- **Data Collection:** Feed the chatbot with data to help it learn how customers phrase their questions.

- **Continuous Training:** Use feedback and real customer conversations to improve accuracy over time.

- **Test for Edge Cases**: Ensure that the bot can handle unexpected or ambiguous inputs without causing frustration.

6. Integrate the Chatbot into Channels

After the chatbot is developed and tested, integrate it into various communication channels:

- **Websites:** Embed the chatbot on your website or landing pages.

- **Mobile Apps:** Implement the chatbot into your mobile application for seamless customer service.

- **Messaging Platforms:** Integrate the chatbot into popular messaging platforms like Facebook Messenger, WhatsApp, or Slack for easy access by customers.

- **Voice Assistants:** For businesses that require voice interactions, consider integrating with voice platforms like Amazon Alexa or Google Assistant.

7. Monitor and Optimize the Chatbot

Post-launch, it's crucial to monitor the chatbot's performance and continually optimize it:

- **Track Key Metrics:** Measure response times, resolution rates, and user satisfaction (via feedback or ratings).

- **Identify Pain Points:** Look for areas where users are frequently unsatisfied or where the chatbot fails to meet expectations.

- **Regular Updates:** Based on user feedback, add new intents, improve the bot's understanding, and update the knowledge base regularly.

8. Add Human Escalation Options

Although AI-powered chatbots are useful for handling repetitive queries, there will always be situations that require human intervention:

- **Seamless Handover:** Ensure that the chatbot can escalate issues to a human agent when it detects a complex query or when it's unable to resolve an issue.

- **Hybrid Approach:** Some chatbots are designed with a hybrid approach, where they start the conversation and collect essential data, but human agents step in for more complex issues.

9. Test and Launch

Before going live, perform extensive testing:

- **User Testing:** Allow real users to interact with the chatbot and provide feedback.

- **Performance Testing:** Ensure that the bot can handle a high volume of requests without performance degradation.

- **Security Testing:** If your chatbot deals with sensitive data (e.g., payment info), ensure proper security measures are in place.
Once you've tested and refined the bot, it's time to launch it and monitor its performance continuously.

10. Measure Success and Iterate

After launching, continuously measure the success of the chatbot against KPIs such as:

- **Customer Satisfaction:** Monitor customer feedback to gauge satisfaction.

- **Reduction in Support Tickets:** Track how many queries are being resolved by the bot instead of requiring human agents.

- **Return on Investment (ROI):** Measure how much time and cost the chatbot has saved for the business.
Based on these metrics, keep refining the chatbot to make it even more effective.

Final Thoughts

Developing an AI-powered chatbot for customer service automation is a process that involves careful planning, the right technology, continuous training, and integration with existing systems. By following these steps, you can create a chatbot that helps businesses improve customer support, enhance user experience, and reduce operational costs

Chapter 20

Data Science & Analytics

Starting a Data Science & Analytics business can be a lucrative and impactful venture, given the increasing demand for data-driven decision-making across industries. Here's a structured approach to help you get started:

1. Identify Your Niche and Market Focus

The field of data science and analytics is vast. To differentiate your business and stand out, you'll need to identify a niche or specific industry where your expertise can deliver the most value. Potential focus areas include:

 - **Industry-specific analytics:** Healthcare, finance, retail, manufacturing, logistics, etc.

 - **Data visualization and reporting:** Helping businesses understand complex data through clear visual representations.

 - **Predictive analytics and forecasting:** Using historical data to make future predictions (e.g., sales forecasts, demand planning).

 - **Machine learning and AI:** Developing custom algorithms to optimize business processes.

 - **Data infrastructure and database management:** Helping companies organize and store data effectively.

 - **Business intelligence (BI):** Helping companies integrate and analyze data from different sources for actionable insights.

2. Build Your Skill set and Expertise

To offer value to your clients, you need a solid foundation in:

 - **Data Analysis:** Proficiency in tools like Excel, SQL, and statistical software (e.g., R, Python, SAS).

 - **Machine Learning:** Knowledge of machine learning algorithms, frameworks (like TensorFlow, PyTorch), and deployment.

- **Data Visualization:** Proficiency in tools such as Tableau, Power BI, or D3.js to present data clearly.

- **Big Data Technologies:** Familiarity with Hadoop, Spark, and cloud platforms like AWS, Google Cloud, or Azure.

- **Data Engineering:** Knowledge of database design, ETL processes, and data warehousing.

- **Business Acumen:** Understanding business processes and objectives to translate data into actionable insights.

3. Market Research and Understanding Your Customers

- **Target Audience:** Identify the types of companies that need data science services. Small to medium-sized enterprises (SMEs), large corporations, and startups may all be potential clients, but they will have different needs and budgets.

- **Pain Points:** Understand what problems companies face in terms of data. For example, they may need help cleaning and organizing their data, predicting trends, or improving their marketing strategies through analytics.

- **Competitor Analysis:** Look at other analytics firms to understand their offerings, pricing, and value propositions. Identify any gaps you can exploit.

4. Business Model and Services

Develop a clear business model that outlines how you will offer services to clients. Common service models include:

- **Consulting:** Providing strategic advice and actionable insights from data analysis.

- **Project-based Work:** Offering tailored analytics solutions for specific business needs.

- **Managed Services:** Offering ongoing data analytics support for a fixed monthly fee.

- **Software-as-a-Service (SaaS):** Developing and selling analytics software or tools.

5. Legal and Administrative Setup

   - **Business Structure:** Choose a legal structure (e.g., LLC, sole proprietorship, corporation) depending on your location and the scope of your business.

   - **Licensing and Permits:** Check if your state or country requires any special licenses for running a data analytics business.

   - **Insurance:** Consider business liability insurance to protect your company from potential legal issues.

   - **Accounting and Tax Setup:** Hire an accountant or use accounting software to keep track of income, expenses, and taxes.

6. Building a Strong Portfolio

   - **Develop Case Studies:** If you're starting without a track record, consider offering free or discounted work to build a portfolio.
   - **Showcase Your Skills:** Use platforms like GitHub, Kaggle, or personal websites to showcase your work. Include example projects, reports, or even small tools that you've built to demonstrate your expertise.
   - **Get Testimonials:** As you start working with clients, ask them for testimonials or case studies that you can use to market your services.

7. Marketing and Client Acquisition

   - **Website:** Create a professional website with a clear value proposition, services offered, and a portfolio of work.

  - **Social Media:** Use LinkedIn, Twitter, and other platforms to share insights, case studies, and industry knowledge. This can help position you as an expert.

   - **Content Marketing:** Write blogs, create videos, or host webinars to educate your audience about the power of data analytics and why they need it.

 - **Networking:** Attend industry conferences, local meetups, and online forums to meet potential clients and partners.

  - **Referral Programs:** Consider implementing a referral program where existing clients or contacts get a reward for referring new customers.

8. Hiring and Team Building

As your business grows, you may need to hire additional talent to scale up. Look for people with complementary skills such as:
- Data scientists with expertise in specific domains (e.g., NLP, computer vision).
- Data engineers to help with data infrastructure.
- Business analysts to help with interpreting data and aligning it with business needs.
- Sales and marketing professionals to help with client acquisition.

9. Tools and Technologies

Invest in the right tools and technologies to run your business efficiently:

- **Project Management Tools:** Tools like Asana, Trello, or Monday.com can help you track progress and deadlines for client projects.

- **Data Analysis Tools:** Keep your team well-equipped with popular software like Python, R, Jupyter notebooks, and relevant libraries (Pandas, NumPy, Scikit-learn).

- **Collaboration Tools:** Use tools like Slack, Google Workspace, or Microsoft Teams for team communication and collaboration.

- **CRM Tools:** Tools like HubSpot or Salesforce can help you manage leads, contacts, and clients.

10. Scaling Your Business

- **Automate and Streamline Processes:** As you grow, automate tasks like data collection, reporting, and client communications to save time and focus on higher-value tasks.

- **Expand Your Offerings:** As you gain experience, expand your offerings to include more advanced services like custom AI solutions, cloud-based analytics, or business intelligence platforms.

- **Outsource or Partner:** Consider outsourcing certain tasks or partnering with other firms that specialize in areas outside your expertise (e.g., app development, advanced machine learning).

11. Continuous Learning and Staying Ahead

The world of data science is evolving rapidly. It's important to:
- Stay updated with the latest trends in AI, machine learning, and big data technologies.
- Attend industry conferences, take courses, and read research papers to continually expand your knowledge.
- Network with other professionals to exchange ideas and explore new business opportunities.

Final Thoughts

Starting a data science and analytics business involves more than just technical skills, it requires strategic planning, a deep understanding of your target market, and a focus on delivering tangible results for clients. With the right skills, a strong portfolio, and a focused marketing strategy, you can position yourself as a valuable partner to companies looking to harness the power of data for better decision-making.

Chapter 21

Cybersecurity Services

Starting a **cybersecurity services business** is a smart and lucrative opportunity in today's digital world, where cyber threats and data breaches are on the rise. Here's a step-by-step guide to help you start your own cybersecurity services business:

1. Conduct Market Research

Before launching your cybersecurity business, it's essential to understand the market demand and competition. Research your target audience—whether it's small businesses, large enterprises, or individuals—and identify the types of cybersecurity services that are in high demand, such as:

- Threat monitoring and detection

- Risk assessments

- Penetration testing

- Network security

- Compliance auditing

- Data encryption and backup solutions

Tip: Focus on a niche market that aligns with your expertise or interests to stand out.

2. Develop a Business Plan

A well-thought-out business plan is crucial for setting the foundation of your cybersecurity business. Your plan should cover the following key areas:

- **Business Name & Structure:** Decide on a catchy and professional business name. Also, choose the business structure (LLC, corporation, sole proprietorship) based on legal, financial, and tax considerations.

- **Service Offerings:** Clearly define what specific services you will offer. This could include consulting, managed security services (MSS), incident response, or compliance assistance for industries like finance, healthcare, or government.

- **Target Audience:** Identify the specific industries or businesses you plan to serve. Different industries may require specialized services or expertise.

- **Marketing & Sales Strategy:** Plan how you will attract customers (e.g., digital marketing, word-of-mouth, networking, industry conferences).

- **Financial Plan:** Include projected startup costs, pricing strategy, and revenue forecasts. Consider your pricing model—hourly rates, subscription services, or project-based pricing.

3. Acquire the Necessary Skills & Certifications

Cybersecurity is a highly specialized field, so it's important to have the technical expertise and credentials to build credibility with potential clients. Some key steps to consider:

- **Get Certified:** Obtain certifications such as Certified Information Systems Security Professional (CISSP), Certified Ethical Hacker (CEH), CompTIA Security+, or Certified Information Security Manager (CISM). These credentials will show your expertise and commitment to best practices.

- **Hands-on Experience:** If you don't already have experience in cybersecurity, gain practical knowledge through internships, freelance work, or by working in IT security roles.

4. Set Up Your Business Infrastructure

Running a cybersecurity services business requires both technical and administrative resources. Consider the following:

- **Office Setup:** Decide whether you'll have a physical office or run the business remotely. Many cybersecurity firms operate entirely online, offering services remotely, which can help reduce overhead costs.

- **Website & Branding:** Develop a professional website that clearly explains your services, expertise, and client testimonials. Make sure your brand communicates trust and security.

- **Tools & Software:** Invest in industry-standard cybersecurity tools for vulnerability scanning, intrusion detection, and threat management. You'll need software for network monitoring, incident response, and compliance reporting.

- **Legal & Regulatory Compliance:** Consult with a lawyer to ensure your business complies with relevant data protection and cybersecurity laws (such as GDPR, CCPA, or HIPAA). Consider drafting contracts and service-level agreements (SLAs) for clients.

5. Build a Network & Develop Partnerships

Cybersecurity is a field that thrives on strong relationships. Building a robust network of professionals can lead to valuable partnerships, referrals, and collaborations.

- Collaborate with Other IT Providers: Partnering with managed IT service providers (MSPs) or software development companies can help you offer complementary services to your clients.

- Attend Industry Events: Cybersecurity conferences, workshops, and local business networking events are great places to meet potential clients and stay updated on industry trends.

- Referral Program: Establish a referral program where clients or partners can earn discounts or other incentives for bringing in new business.

6. Market Your Services

Effective marketing is critical to attracting clients. Here's how you can promote your cybersecurity services:

- Content Marketing: Create blogs, whitepapers, or videos on cybersecurity topics like best practices, threat intelligence, and case studies to establish thought leadership.

- Social Media & SEO: Use social media platforms like LinkedIn, Twitter, and Instagram to share cybersecurity tips and industry news. Invest in SEO to ensure your website ranks high in search results for relevant queries like "cybersecurity services" or "data breach protection."

- Paid Advertising: Consider running paid ads on Google or LinkedIn to target businesses looking for cybersecurity services.

- Client Testimonials & Case Studies: Showcase positive feedback and successful case studies to build trust with potential customers.

7. Start Small, Scale Gradually

Initially, you may want to start small, offering your services to local businesses or startups. As you build a solid reputation and customer base, you can gradually scale up your services and expand your target market.

- Start with a Few Clients: Focus on delivering high-quality service to your first clients. A few successful projects can generate word-of-mouth referrals.

- **Outsource or Hire:** As your business grows, you may need to hire additional staff or outsource certain functions, such as marketing, administrative tasks, or advanced technical services.

8. Stay Updated on Emerging Cyber Threats

The world of cybersecurity evolves rapidly. Keep yourself and your team up-to-date on the latest security trends, vulnerabilities, and technologies by:

- **Attending Webinars and Conferences:** Stay informed about emerging cyber threats and best practices.

- **Regular Training:** Continuously improve your team's skills through training programs and certifications to stay ahead of the curve.

9. Ensure High-Quality Customer Support

Cybersecurity is a service that often requires ongoing support. Offering strong customer service can set you apart from competitors. Provide:

- **24/7 Support:** Some clients may need urgent assistance at any time of the day or night.

- **Clear Communication:** Regular check-ins, security reports, and updates are essential to maintaining trust with your clients.

- **Incident Response:** Be ready to provide quick and efficient incident response services in case of a breach or security threat.

Final Thoughts

Starting a cybersecurity services business requires a mix of technical expertise, business acumen, and an understanding of market demands. By following the steps outlined above—conducting research, acquiring certifications, building a solid business plan, and marketing effectively—you can position your business for growth in this thriving, high-demand industry. With a strong foundation in both security and customer service, you'll be well on your way to building a successful cybersecurity business that helps protect your clients from ever-evolving digital threats.

Chapter 22

Software as a Service (SaaS)

1. Identify a Target Industry and Niche

- **Research & Identify Pain Points:** Start by researching industries that could benefit from software solutions. Look for pain points or inefficiencies that are currently underserved by existing software solutions. This could be anything from operational bottlenecks to compliance challenges or customer relationship management.

- **Choose a Niche:** While targeting an entire industry can be tempting, focusing on a specific niche within an industry will allow you to tailor your offering to a more specific set of problems. For example, if you are targeting healthcare, you could focus on clinic management or telehealth software.

- **Assess Market Demand:** Validate the need for your SaaS product by talking to potential users, conducting surveys, or evaluating competitor solutions. This helps ensure there's enough demand for the software you're planning to build.

2. Develop a Business Plan

- **Value Proposition:** Define the core problem your software solves and why your solution is better than current alternatives. Make it clear why your SaaS solution is unique and what differentiates it from competitors.

- **Revenue Model:** As you're focusing on a subscription-based model, decide on pricing tiers based on your target market's budget. Common pricing structures include:

  - **Freemium Model:** Offer basic features for free, charging for advanced features.

  - **Tiered Pricing:** Offer different pricing levels based on features, user count, or usage limits.

  - **Flat-rate Pricing:** Charge a fixed monthly or annual fee.

- **Financial Projections:** Estimate your expected income, costs, and break-even point. This should include costs for product development, marketing, staffing, hosting infrastructure, etc.

3. Build the Minimum Viable Product (MVP)

- **Focus on Core Features:** Build the MVP with only the essential features that solve the identified pain points in your target industry. The goal is to create a functional product that can be tested and iterated upon.

- **Choose the Right Technology Stack:** Pick technologies that align with your product's needs. Consider scalability, security, and integration with other tools commonly used in the industry.

- **User Experience (UX) Design:** SaaS products often have complex workflows, so prioritize a user-friendly interface that streamlines the user experience.

- **Cloud Infrastructure:** Host your product on reliable cloud platforms like AWS, Google Cloud, or Azure. Make sure your infrastructure can scale as the user base grows.

4. Set Up Subscription and Payment System

- **Subscription Management Tools:** Integrate with a subscription management platform (e.g., Stripe, Chargebee, or Recurly) to handle recurring billing, invoicing, and payment processing.

- **Trial Period:** Offer a free trial period (e.g., 14-30 days) to allow users to experience the value of your software before committing to a paid subscription.

- **Pricing Pages:** Design clear, easy-to-understand pricing pages that highlight the value of each subscription tier and encourage sign-ups.

5. Develop a Go-to-Market Strategy

- **Create a Website:** Build a professional website with a clear value proposition, product features, customer testimonials, and a simple sign-up process.

- **Marketing:**

  - **Content Marketing:** Start a blog, publish case studies, and produce industry-specific content that educates your target audience on the benefits of your software.

  - **SEO:** Optimize your website for search engines to drive organic traffic. Target long-tail keywords relevant to the industry you're serving.

  - **Paid Advertising:** Run targeted ads on platforms like Google Ads, LinkedIn, or industry-specific sites.

  - **Outbound Sales:** Consider building an outbound sales team to contact potential leads via email, cold calls, or social media outreach.

- Partnerships: Build partnerships with industry influencers, trade organizations, or complementary software providers to expand your reach.

6. Acquire Early Adopters and Feedback

   - Beta Testing: Release your MVP to a small group of beta testers to gather feedback on usability, bugs, and overall experience. Use this feedback to improve the product.

   - Customer Feedback Loop: Continuously engage with users to collect feedback on new features, improvements, and areas that need attention. Use tools like surveys or in-app feedback widgets.

   - Community Building: Create forums, online communities, or support channels where users can interact with each other and provide feedback.

7. Customer Support & Retention

   - Onboarding: Create an easy-to-follow onboarding process to help users get started quickly. Offer tutorials, guides, and videos to facilitate adoption.

   - Customer Support: Provide excellent customer support through multiple channels such as live chat, email, and phone. Consider implementing a help desk platform like Zendesk or Intercom.

   - Churn Reduction: Monitor customer engagement metrics and act on signs of churn. Offer incentives, personalized outreach, or product improvements to retain users.

8. Scale & Iterate

   - Feature Development: Based on user feedback and market trends, continue to add valuable features to your SaaS product. Make sure you're addressing evolving industry needs.

  - Infrastructure Scaling: As your customer base grows, ensure your infrastructure can handle the increased demand. Invest in scalable cloud services and monitor system performance.

   - Expansion: After gaining traction in one niche, consider expanding to other segments or regions within the industry. You may also explore vertical integration (offering more products within your SaaS suite) to increase lifetime value.

9. Monitor Key Metrics & Optimize

- **Key Performance Indicators (KPIs):** Track important SaaS metrics such as Monthly Recurring Revenue (MRR), Customer Acquisition Cost (CAC), Customer Lifetime Value (CLTV), churn rate, and user engagement.

- **A/B Testing:** Use A/B testing for features, marketing campaigns, and pricing to find the most effective strategies for driving growth and customer retention.

- **Continuous Improvement:** Regularly review your performance, seek customer feedback, and update your product and business strategy accordingly to optimize growth and profitability.

Final Thoughts

Starting a SaaS business in a specific industry requires a combination of deep market understanding, a well-defined product offering, effective customer acquisition strategies, and strong operational execution. By focusing on a niche, building a user-friendly product, and adopting a subscription-based model, you can position your business for long-term success. Focus on delivering value to your users, and iterate based on feedback to keep improving your product and business strategy.

Chapter 23

3D Printing Business

Starting a 3D printing business offering custom-designed items such as prototypes, parts, or art can be an exciting and profitable venture. To help you get started, here's a step-by-step guide:

1. Conduct Market Research

Before diving into your 3D printing business, it's crucial to understand your target market. Identify industries or niches that might need custom 3D printing services. Some potential areas include:

- **Product design & prototyping:** Small businesses or inventors who need to create prototypes of their products.

- **Manufacturing:** Companies in need of custom parts or tools.

- **Art & Design:** Artists and hobbyists interested in creating one-of-a-kind sculptures, jewelry, or custom artwork.

- **Education and Healthcare:** Schools, universities, or medical institutions needing 3D-printed educational models or custom medical devices.

Research competitors, pricing, demand, and what differentiates your business. This will help shape your services and marketing strategies.

2. Define Your Business Model and Niche

3D printing can cover a wide range of industries and applications. Narrowing down your niche will make it easier to market your services effectively. Consider:
- **Prototyping:** Offering fast, reliable, and affordable prototypes for engineers, designers, or inventors.

- **Small Batch Production:** Focusing on producing small batches of custom parts or products for clients.

- **Art & Design:** Creating personalized art pieces, sculptures, jewelry, or home decor.

- **Education & Training:** Providing 3D-printed models or tools for educational purposes.

- **Customization Services:** Custom printing for individuals (e.g., personalized items like phone cases, trophies, etc.).

Choosing a specific niche will help define your brand, target audience, and the types of 3D printers and materials you should invest in.

3. Develop a Business Plan

A solid business plan is essential to outline the details of your business and ensure its long-term success. Your plan should cover:

- **Services Offered:** Describe the specific 3D printing services you will offer.

- **Target Market:** Identify your target audience and industries you plan to serve.

- **Marketing Strategy:** How will you promote your services? Consider online platforms (social media, SEO, online marketplaces) and offline strategies (networking events, local advertising).

- **Pricing Model:** Set competitive pricing based on market research, costs, and the value of your services.

- **Equipment and Materials:** Identify the types of 3D printers, materials (PLA, ABS, resin, etc.), and software you will need.

- **Financial Projections:** Estimate startup costs, revenue, and profit margins.

4. Invest in Equipment and Software

To deliver high-quality 3D printing services, invest in the right equipment and software. Your needs will vary based on the types of services you plan to offer:

- **3D Printers:** There are several types of 3D printers, such as FDM (Fused Deposition Modeling), SLA (Stereolithography), and SLS (Selective Laser Sintering). FDM printers are popular for prototyping and parts, while SLA printers are ideal for highly detailed models and art.

- **Materials:** Choose materials based on your niche. Common materials include PLA, ABS, resin, PETG, and flexible filaments.

- **Design Software:** Software like AutoCAD, Blender, or Fusion 360 is essential for creating and modifying 3D models.
- Post-Processing Equipment: Depending on your service offering, you may need additional tools for cleaning, curing, or finishing prints.

Consider the initial investment carefully and choose equipment that balances cost and quality. As your business grows, you can upgrade to more specialized machines.

5. Legal Considerations

Before launching your 3D printing business, ensure that you have the necessary legal and financial groundwork:

- **Business Structure:** Decide whether to operate as a sole proprietor, partnership, or limited liability company (LLC). An LLC offers personal liability protection.

- **Licenses & Permits:** Depending on your location, you may need a business license and local permits to operate a 3D printing service.

- **Insurance:** Protect your business with liability insurance in case of damage to clients' products or other liabilities.

- **Intellectual Property (IP) Considerations:** If you're creating original designs, make sure to understand copyright, patent, and trademark laws. If printing designs for clients, clarify ownership of the final product.

6. Build an Online Presence

A strong online presence is key for attracting customers. Some important steps to take:

- **Website:** Create a professional website showcasing your services, portfolio, pricing, and contact information. You can include a gallery of your work and even offer online ordering or design submission features.

- **Social Media:** Use platforms like Instagram, Facebook, and LinkedIn to showcase your work. Post videos of the printing process, client success stories, and educational content related to 3D printing.

- **SEO & Content Marketing:** Optimize your website for search engines to attract organic traffic. Write blogs, guides, and tutorials related to 3D printing to engage potential clients.

- **Online Marketplaces:** Consider listing your products or services on platforms like Etsy, Shapeways, or 3D Hubs, which can help you reach a larger audience.

7. Launch and Promote Your Business

Once you have everything set up, it's time to launch your business:

- **Soft Launch:** Start by offering your services to a small group of people—friends, family, or initial clients. Gather feedback to refine your offerings.

- **Promotional Offers:** To build momentum, offer discounts, free consultations, or package deals for your first few customers.

- **Networking:** Attend trade shows, maker fairs, or local business networking events to meet potential clients. Join online communities, forums, and groups focused on 3D printing to expand your reach.

- **Customer Reviews & Referrals:** Ask satisfied customers for testimonials and encourage them to refer others to your business.

8. Monitor & Scale Your Business

As you gain experience and expand your customer base, regularly review your performance:

- **Customer Feedback:** Continually seek feedback to improve your services and product quality.

- **Analyze Financials:** Keep track of expenses, revenue, and profits to ensure your business is financially sustainable.

- **Expand Offerings:** As demand grows, you can add more services (e.g., larger prints, custom designs) or invest in more advanced printers for specific materials.

- **Automation & Efficiency:** Look for ways to streamline production, automate design submissions, or speed up post-processing.

Starting a 3D printing business can be an exciting journey with a lot of creative and commercial potential. With the right tools, strategy, and dedication, you can carve out a successful niche in this fast-evolving industry.

Chapter 24

16. Tech Support for Small Businesses

Starting a **Tech Support Business for Small Businesses** is a great way to tap into a growing demand for affordable IT services. Many small businesses need reliable tech support but can't afford to hire full-time IT staff. By offering freelance or contract-based IT services, you can meet this need while building a flexible, scalable business.

Here's a step-by-step guide to help you start:

1. Identify Your Niche & Services

Small businesses have diverse tech needs, so it's essential to identify which services you will offer. Common IT support services include:

- Network setup & maintenance

- Hardware and software troubleshooting

- Data backups & recovery

- Cybersecurity protection & monitoring

- Cloud solutions & email management

- Remote tech support

- Tech training for employees

You can choose to specialize in one or more areas depending on your expertise and market demand. Understanding your niche helps you target the right clients and differentiate yourself from competitors.

2. Conduct Market Research

Research your local market to understand the demand for tech support services and what businesses need. Key questions to ask include:

- Which small businesses in your area rely on technology but can't afford full-time IT staff?

- What are the most common tech challenges they face?

- Who are your competitors, and what services do they offer?

- How much can small businesses afford to pay for tech support?

Market research helps you tailor your offerings and price your services competitively.

3. Create a Business Plan

A solid business plan is crucial for guiding your business and securing clients. Include the following elements:

- **Executive Summary:** What your business does and your mission.

- **Market Analysis**: Insights from your research on demand, competitors, and target customers.

- **Services and Pricing:** List of services, pricing structure (hourly rate, fixed pricing, retainer, etc.).

- **Marketing Strategy:** How you'll promote your services (online marketing, networking, word of mouth).

- **Financial Projections:** Estimated startup costs, expected revenue, and profitability.

- **Goals:** Short-term and long-term goals for growing your business.

4. Legal Structure and Business Setup

Determine the legal structure of your business. Common options include:

- **Sole Proprietorship:** Simple to set up, but you're personally responsible for liabilities.

- **LLC (Limited Liability Company):** Provides personal liability protection and may offer tax advantages.

- **S-Corp:** Suitable for larger businesses with multiple employees, allowing for pass-through taxation.

Register your business with local authorities, and obtain any necessary licenses or permits. You may also want to set up business insurance to protect yourself and your clients.

5. Set Up Your Equipment and Tools

You'll need a range of tools to provide effective tech support. Consider investing in:

- **Remote support software** (e.g., TeamViewer, AnyDesk)

- **Diagnostic tools** for hardware troubleshooting

- **Cloud storage solutions** for data backup

- **Antivirus & cybersecurity software**

- **Accounting & invoicing tools** (e.g., QuickBooks, FreshBooks)

Additionally, make sure you have a reliable laptop, high-speed internet, and any other necessary IT equipment.

6. Build an Online Presence

Many small businesses start their search for IT support online, so it's essential to have a professional online presence:

- **Create a website:** Outline your services, provide testimonials, and include a contact form.

- **Social Media:** Set up business profiles on LinkedIn, Facebook, and Twitter to promote your services and engage with potential clients.

- **Google My Business:** Register your business to appear in local searches and reviews.

- **Online Reviews:** Ask satisfied clients to leave reviews on platforms like Google or Yelp to build credibility.

7. Start Networking and Generating Leads

Building a client base for a freelance tech support business often comes down to networking. Consider:

- **Reaching out to local businesses:** Offer a free consultation or discounted first service to build trust.

- **Joining local business organizations:** Such as chambers of commerce or small business groups.

- **Referral programs:** Offer incentives for clients who refer other small businesses to you.

- **Cold emailing or calling:** Reach out to potential clients directly to introduce yourself and explain your services.

Word-of-mouth marketing is powerful, so aim to build relationships with clients and deliver excellent service.

8. Set Your Pricing Structure

Determine how you'll charge for your services. There are several common pricing models:

- **Hourly Rate:** Ideal for troubleshooting or one-time services.

- **Monthly Retainer:** A fixed monthly fee for ongoing support, which offers predictable income.

- **Per-Project Pricing:** Charging a flat fee for a specific task, like setting up a new server or migrating data.

- **Remote vs. On-Site Support:** You may charge different rates based on whether you're providing remote or on-site services.

Make sure your pricing is competitive but also reflective of your expertise and the value you provide.

9. Develop a Client Onboarding Process

A smooth onboarding process is crucial for client retention. When a new client hires you, outline:

- What services they'll receive.

- How you'll communicate (email, phone, in-person visits).

- The expected response time for support requests.

- Payment terms and billing frequency.

A well-organized process builds professionalism and trust from the start.

10. Continually Improve and Scale Your Business

As you gain more experience and clients, consider expanding your service offerings, hiring employees or subcontractors, or even offering specialized services (e.g., cybersecurity consulting, cloud migration).

Invest in ongoing training to stay up-to-date with the latest technology trends, tools, and best practices. Building a reputation as a knowledgeable and reliable tech support provider will help you grow your business over time.

Final Thoughts

Starting a tech support business for small businesses can be a highly rewarding venture. By offering affordable, flexible, and expert IT solutions, you'll become a valuable resource for companies that rely on technology but can't justify the expense of an in-house IT team. With the right planning, marketing, and customer service, you can build a thriving freelance tech support business that helps small businesses stay up and running smoothly.

Chapter 25

Drone Services

Starting a drone services business can be a lucrative venture, given the wide range of industries that are increasingly adopting drone technology. Whether you're interested in offering drone photography, surveying, agricultural services, or other applications, here's a step-by-step guide to help you get started.

1. Research the Market and Identify Your Niche

Before you launch your drone services business, you need to understand the market. Drones can be used across a variety of industries, so it's crucial to identify the specific services you want to offer. Some popular niches include:

- **Aerial Photography & Videography:** Offering services for real estate, events, marketing, and film production.

- **Surveying & Mapping:** Using drones for land surveying, construction, and engineering projects.

- **Agriculture:** Providing crop monitoring, precision agriculture, and land management solutions.

- **Inspection Services:** Drones for inspecting infrastructure such as power lines, wind turbines, bridges, and buildings.

- **Environmental Monitoring:** Wildlife surveys, environmental impact assessments, and forest management.

2. Get the Necessary Qualifications and Certifications

In most countries, operating drones for commercial purposes requires meeting regulatory requirements and obtaining the appropriate certifications. This is especially true for certain industries like surveying, agriculture, and inspections.

- **FAA Part 107 Certification (U.S.):** In the U.S., to operate drones commercially, you need to pass the FAA Part 107 exam, which covers drone operation rules, airspace regulations, weather, and other safety topics.

- **Local Aviation Authority:** If you're in another country, check with your national aviation authority for drone operation rules.

- **Insurance:** Consider drone insurance that covers damage to your drone, liability, and any potential accidents that might occur while flying.

3. Invest in Equipment and Technology

The type of drones and technology you need will depend on the services you're offering. Here are some of the key factors to consider:

- **Drones:** Invest in high-quality drones that are suited for your niche. For example, you might need a drone with high-definition cameras for photography or a more rugged drone with thermal sensors for inspections. Some popular drones for commercial use include:

  - **DJI Phantom 4 RTK** (for surveying)

  - **DJI Matrice 300 RTK** (for inspections)

  - **DJI Mavic 3** (for photography and video)

- **Software:** You'll need specialized software for flight planning, image processing, and analysis. For example:

  - **Pix4D** for mapping and surveying

  - **DroneDeploy** for flight planning and mapping

  - **Agremo** or **Sentera** for agricultural applications

- **Accessories**: Spare batteries, controllers, and other equipment are essential to ensure you can operate efficiently.

4. Create a Business Plan

A business plan is critical to map out your strategy, goals, and financial projections. Consider the following when creating your business plan:

- **Market Research:** Understand your competitors, target audience, and pricing strategies.

- **Revenue Model:** Define how you'll generate income. For example, you could charge hourly rates, offer packages, or create subscription-based services for clients.

- **Marketing and Sales:** Outline your marketing plan, which might include a website, social media campaigns, attending industry events, and networking with potential clients.

- **Expenses:** Consider initial investment costs (drones, equipment, insurance, software), ongoing costs (maintenance, marketing, employee wages), and expected revenue.

5. Register Your Business and Legal Considerations

- **Business Structure:** Decide on the legal structure of your business. Common options include sole proprietorship, limited liability company (LLC), or corporation.

- **Business License:** Obtain any necessary business licenses or permits required in your area.

- **Taxes:** Set up your tax structure, including sales tax (if applicable) and income tax. It's a good idea to consult a tax professional.

- **Liability Insurance:** Drone operations involve risks, so having liability insurance can protect your business from potential lawsuits or damages caused during flight operations.

6. Build Your Portfolio and Online Presence
A strong portfolio and online presence will help attract clients and establish credibility in the industry.

- **Website:** Create a professional website showcasing your services, portfolio of work (including aerial photos/videos), pricing, and contact details.

- **Social Media:** Use platforms like Instagram, YouTube, and LinkedIn to share your work and engage with potential clients.

- **Client Testimonials:** Gather testimonials from satisfied clients to build trust with future prospects.

- **Drone Job Platforms:** Register with online platforms like DroneBase, Upwork, or others that connect drone operators with clients.

7. Market Your Drone Services

Effective marketing strategies are crucial for getting your business off the ground.

- **Local Networking:** Attend local events, trade shows, or business expos related to industries that use drones.

- **Content Marketing:** Publish blog posts, videos, or case studies showcasing how your drone services can benefit businesses in specific industries.

- **Google Ads & Social Media Advertising:** Use targeted ads to attract potential clients in your service area. Ads on platforms like Google, Facebook, and Instagram can help you reach specific demographics.

- **Collaborations:** Partner with other businesses in your niche (real estate agents, construction companies, etc.) to provide bundled services.

8. Focus on Customer Service and Building Relationships

The key to long-term success is not just attracting new clients but also retaining them. Focus on:

- **Delivering Quality:** Ensure that your drone work is high quality, whether it's photography, mapping, or inspection.

- **Clear Communication:** Keep clients informed about your process and ensure that they understand what to expect from your services.

- **Follow-Up:** After completing a project, follow up with clients to ensure satisfaction and ask for referrals or testimonials.

9. Scale Your Business

Once your business starts to generate consistent revenue, you can look into expanding:

- **Hiring:** Consider hiring other drone operators or office staff to handle administrative work, allowing you to focus on growing your business.

- **Service Expansion:** Add new services (e.g., thermal inspections, LiDAR mapping, or 3D modeling) or expand into other regions or industries.

- **Upgrade Equipment:** As your business grows, invest in more advanced drones and equipment to meet the demands of larger projects or specialized applications.

Final Thoughts

Starting a drone services business can be a rewarding and profitable venture if you take the time to plan, get the proper certifications, invest in the right equipment, and effectively market your services. With drones becoming more integrated into industries like real estate, agriculture, construction, and film, there's no shortage of opportunities for innovation and growth in this space.

Chapter 26

Virtual Reality Experiences

Starting a Virtual Reality (VR) Experiences business, particularly focused on building VR platforms or games that offer unique experiences, is an exciting and rapidly evolving opportunity. Here's a step-by-step guide to help you plan and execute your business effectively:

1. Identify Your Niche and Target Audience

   - **Target Market:** Start by defining the type of VR experiences you'll provide. Will your focus be on consumers (gaming, entertainment, education, travel) or businesses (corporate training, real estate, virtual events)?

   - **Market Research:** Research the demand within your chosen niche. Look for gaps in existing VR offerings, whether it's a particular type of game, simulation, or experience that is underserved.

   - **Unique Selling Proposition (USP):** What makes your VR platform or game different from competitors? It could be better graphics, interactivity, storylines, or an innovative use of VR technology.

2. Business Model and Monetization

   - **Types of VR Experiences:** Decide whether you'll focus on creating:

     - **Games:** VR games for entertainment and leisure.

     - **Training Platforms:** Simulations for corporate or educational training.

     - **Experiential Platforms:** VR experiences for retail, tourism, virtual tourism, or art exhibitions.

     - **Events and Social VR:** Creating platforms for virtual meetings, conventions, or multiplayer social VR.

   - **Monetization Options:**

     - **Subscription Model:** Charge users a recurring fee to access your VR content.

     - **One-Time Purchase:** Sell the VR games or experiences as standalone products.

- **Freemium Model:** Offer a free experience with the option to purchase premium features or content.

   - **Licensing and B2B:** License your VR platform or technology to businesses in industries like education, healthcare, or real estate.

3. Create a Business Plan

   - **Executive Summary:** Outline your business goals, mission, and vision for the VR experience platform.

   - **Technology and Development:** Define the technical specifications and tools you'll need to build your VR products.

   - **Financial Plan:** Estimate startup costs, including hardware, software development, and marketing. Forecast revenue, growth, and break-even points.

   - **Marketing and Sales Strategy:** Plan how you'll reach your target audience—through social media, online communities, VR events, or influencer partnerships.

   - **Team:** Identify the key roles you need to fill, including VR developers, artists, designers, and possibly business development or marketing experts.

4. Develop Your VR Platform/Game

   - **Choose a Development Tool/Engine:**

   - **Unity:** A popular engine for creating VR games and experiences. It has robust VR development support, and there are plenty of tutorials and resources available.

   - **Unreal Engine:** Known for stunning visuals, Unreal is a great choice if you're looking to create high-quality, immersive experiences.

   - **Hardware Requirements:** Develop for the most common VR hardware, such as Oculus Quest, HTC Vive, or PlayStation VR. Consider supporting multiple platforms to reach a broader audience.

   - **User Experience (UX) and Design:** Focus on creating intuitive interfaces and controls that are easy to use in a VR environment. VR experiences require attention to detail in user comfort, preventing motion sickness, and creating engaging interactions.

5. Develop the Content

- **Story and Interaction:** Whether it's a game or a VR training experience, the content should be engaging. Storytelling and immersive environments are key to retaining users.

- **Graphics and Audio:** High-quality graphics, sound design, and physics are crucial to creating a believable and immersive VR experience.

- **Prototyping and Testing:** Create a prototype and run internal tests before releasing your product. Collect feedback and refine your experience based on that feedback.

6. Marketing and Launching Your VR Experience

- **Create a Website and Branding:** Your website should showcase your VR offerings, provide demos, and allow users to purchase or subscribe. Also, develop a strong visual brand and logo to differentiate your business.

- **Social Media:** Build a community on platforms like Instagram, TikTok, and YouTube. Showcase trailers, behind-the-scenes content, and user experiences. Consider launching a YouTube or Twitch channel to stream gameplay and engage with potential users.

- **Influencer Partnerships:** Partner with VR influencers or streamers to create buzz around your product. Influencers can help showcase the experience to a broader audience.

- **SEO and Content Marketing:** Create engaging content like blogs, videos, or tutorials related to VR, its benefits, and how it's revolutionizing your niche. This will help your site rank on search engines and attract organic traffic.

- **Launch Event:** Consider a virtual launch event or a demo at a VR expo or gaming conference. These types of events can help you gain exposure in the VR industry.

7. Customer Support and Community Engagement

- **Support Channels:** Offer good customer support through email, live chat, or social media channels. Users will appreciate quick assistance, especially when it comes to troubleshooting hardware or software issues.

- **Community Engagement:** Building a community is key to long-term success. Engage with users on forums, social media, and VR spaces to get feedback and foster loyalty.

- **Updates and Expansions:** Regularly release updates, new content, or features to keep users engaged and coming back.

8. Legal and Administrative Considerations

- **Legal Requirements:** Depending on your location, you may need to register your business and obtain necessary licenses. Consult a legal professional to ensure you're complying with any data protection, copyright, and intellectual property laws related to VR content.

- **Partnerships and Contracts:** If you plan to license your VR experiences or work with other businesses, you may need contracts or partnership agreements. Make sure to outline terms for usage rights, royalties, and distribution.

9. Scaling and Future Growth

- **Evaluate Performance:** Monitor the performance of your VR experiences—how many users, sales, and subscriptions are you getting? Use this data to improve and refine your product.

- **Expand Your Offerings:** As your business grows, consider diversifying your VR portfolio by expanding into new industries, creating new experiences, or developing companion apps and devices.

- **Partnerships and Funding:** If you need funding to expand, explore options like venture capital, crowdfunding, or partnerships with larger tech companies.

10. Stay Ahead of the Curve

- **Innovate:** The VR industry is still in its early stages, and technology is evolving rapidly. Stay updated on the latest trends, such as mixed reality (MR), eye-tracking, haptic feedback, and AI-driven interactive experiences.

- **Networking:** Join VR-related industry groups, attend trade shows, and connect with other VR professionals. Being part of the VR community can provide valuable insights, collaborations, and partnerships.

Final Thoughts

Starting a VR experiences business requires a combination of creativity, technical expertise, and a deep understanding of your target audience's needs. By focusing on delivering unique, high-quality VR content, building a strong marketing strategy, and continuously innovating, you can create a successful business in this exciting space.

Chapter 27

Blockchain Development

Starting a blockchain development business can be a highly rewarding venture, especially as blockchain technology continues to mature and find applications in industries like finance, supply chain, healthcare, and more. Here's a step-by-step guide on how to get started:

1. Understand the Blockchain Ecosystem

- **Deepen Your Knowledge:** Before starting a blockchain development business, you need a solid understanding of how blockchain works. This includes knowledge of consensus mechanisms (like Proof of Work, Proof of Stake), smart contracts, decentralized applications (dApps), and various blockchain platforms such as Ethereum, Solana, Polkadot, and others.

- **Stay Updated:** Blockchain is a rapidly evolving field, so keeping up with the latest trends, advancements, and use cases is essential.

2. Identify a Niche or Problem to Solve

- **Target Market:** Decide whether you want to build general-purpose solutions or specialize in a specific industry. Some potential areas include:

  - **Finance:** Decentralized finance (DeFi), tokenization, stablecoins, digital assets.

  - **Supply Chain:** Transparent tracking of goods, proof of provenance.

  - **Healthcare:** Secure patient data management, decentralized health records.

  - **Gaming and NFTs:** Blockchain-based games, non-fungible tokens (NFTs).

  - **Enterprise Solutions:** Smart contracts for business process automation.

- **Market Research:** Understand the pain points of the industry you're targeting. Look for inefficiencies that blockchain technology can address.

3. Build a Strong Technical Team

 - **Skill Sets Needed:**

   - **Blockchain Developers:** Knowledge of blockchain platforms (Ethereum, Binance Smart Chain, Solana, etc.), smart contract development (Solidity, Rust), dApp development, and cryptography.

   - **Front-End Developers:** Expertise in building user-friendly interfaces for dApps.

   - **Back-End Developers:** Knowledge of integrating blockchain with back-end infrastructure.

   - **Security Experts:** Blockchain security is critical; ensure your team includes experts who can audit and secure smart contracts and decentralized systems.

   - **Hiring:** Look for skilled developers, or train your own team. Many developers are learning blockchain skills through online courses, boot camps, and certifications.

4. Decide on the Blockchain Platforms and Tools

   - **Choose the Right Blockchain:** Depending on the use case, you'll need to select the most appropriate blockchain platform (e.g., Ethereum, Hyperledger, Tezos, or Polkadot). Consider factors like scalability, transaction speed, cost, and security.

   - **Development Tools and Frameworks:**

   - **Truffle:** A popular framework for Ethereum development.

   - **Hardhat**: Another development environment for Ethereum smart contracts.

   - **Solidity:** A programming language for writing smart contracts on Ethereum.

   - **IPFS:** For decentralized file storage.

   - **Chainlink**: For decentralized oracles.

5. Legal and Compliance Considerations

   - **Legal Structure:** Register your business according to local regulations. Consider forming an LLC or corporation depending on your jurisdiction.

- **Compliance with Regulations:** Blockchain and cryptocurrency regulations vary by country and region. Make sure you're compliant with the laws regarding:
    - Token issuance (ICOs, STOs).
    - Data privacy laws (e.g., GDPR).
    - Anti-money laundering (AML) and know-your-customer (KYC) regulations.

- **Smart Contract Auditing:** Ensure that any smart contracts you develop are secure and free from vulnerabilities, as bugs can lead to financial losses or legal issues.

6. Develop a Portfolio of Projects

- **Build Proof of Concept (PoC):** Start by creating a few demo projects or dApps to showcase your capabilities. This could include a simple blockchain application like a voting system, token, or supply chain tracker.

- **Create a Website/Portfolio:** Develop a professional website showcasing your team, services, and portfolio of completed blockchain projects. Case studies and testimonials from clients can be powerful tools for attracting new business.

- **Open Source Contributions:** Contribute to open-source blockchain projects. This helps build credibility in the blockchain community and can lead to potential collaborations and clients.

7. Marketing and Networking

- **Leverage Social Media and Content:** Use platforms like Twitter, LinkedIn, Medium, and YouTube to share your expertise, write about blockchain developments, and engage with the community.

- **Join Blockchain Communities:** Participate in blockchain meetups, forums (e.g., Reddit, StackExchange), and attend blockchain conferences. Networking with other developers and business owners can help you stay informed and get your foot in the door for new opportunities.

- **Partnerships:** Collaborate with businesses or startups that could benefit from your blockchain solutions. Building partnerships can help grow your brand and establish credibility in the industry.

8. Funding Your Blockchain Development Business

- **Bootstrapping:** Many blockchain startups begin by self-funding the initial stages until they have built a working product and gained traction.

- **Venture Capital (VC):** As blockchain technology has gained popularity, many venture capitalists are looking to invest in promising blockchain startups. Create a compelling pitch for your business if you're seeking external funding.

- **Grants and Competitions:** Look for blockchain development grants or hackathons. Many blockchain foundations (like Ethereum Foundation, Polkadot) offer funding or rewards for innovative projects.

9. Offer Services Beyond Development

- **Consulting:** Offer consulting services to businesses interested in implementing blockchain but unsure of how to integrate it into their operations.

- **Training:** Blockchain skills are in high demand. You could offer training workshops or online courses to help other businesses upskill their teams.

- **Blockchain as a Service (BaaS):** Provide cloud-based blockchain infrastructure and development tools for businesses that want to build decentralized applications without managing the underlying infrastructure.

10. Focus on Customer Support and Post-Launch Services

- **Maintenance and Updates:** Blockchain networks evolve, and businesses will need ongoing maintenance for their decentralized apps or blockchain solutions. Providing regular updates and ensuring security patches is crucial for client satisfaction.

- **User Education:** Blockchain is still a complex technology for many, so providing educational resources, guides, or direct support to clients will set your business apart.

Final Thoughts

Starting a blockchain development business requires a combination of technical expertise, market insight, and business acumen. By selecting the right niche, building a skilled team, and staying on top of industry trends, you can position your business as a leader in the blockchain space. Given the growing demand for decentralized solutions across various industries, this is a great time to enter the blockchain development market.

Chapter 28

Cloud Computing Services

Starting a cloud computing services business can be an exciting and rewarding venture, given the increasing demand for cloud migration and cloud-based solutions across industries. Here's a step-by-step guide on how you might start a cloud computing services business to help companies migrate to the cloud or offer tailored cloud-based solutions.

1. Identify Your Niche & Value Proposition

The cloud computing market is vast, so narrowing your focus can help you stand out. Consider offering services in one or more of the following areas:

- **Cloud Migration Services:** Help businesses move their data, applications, and operations to the cloud.

- **Cloud-based Industry Solutions:** Provide specialized cloud services for specific industries (e.g., healthcare, retail, finance).

- **Cloud Security Solutions:** Focus on providing secure cloud environments for sensitive data and operations.

- **Cloud Infrastructure Management:** Manage the infrastructure needs of businesses in the cloud, ensuring scalability and optimization.

Define Your Value Proposition: Once you've identified your niche, focus on what makes your services unique. Do you offer faster migration, enhanced security, lower costs, or personalized customer support?

2. Build Expertise and Partnerships

Cloud computing is a highly technical field, so ensuring you or your team has the necessary skills is essential. You might need to:

- **Certifications:** Obtain certifications like AWS Certified Solutions Architect, Google Cloud Professional Cloud Architect, or Microsoft Azure certifications.

- **Technology Partnerships:** Build relationships with major cloud providers like AWS, Microsoft Azure, Google Cloud, or IBM Cloud. This will not only enhance your credibility but also potentially give you access to partner programs, resources, and support.

3. Develop Your Service Offerings

Break down the specific services you'll offer. For instance:

- **Cloud Strategy & Consulting:** Help businesses assess their needs and design a cloud strategy.

- **Cloud Migration & Implementation:** Assist businesses with moving their infrastructure and data to the cloud.

- **Managed Cloud Services:** Provide ongoing management, monitoring, and support for cloud environments.

- **Cloud Optimization & Cost Management:** Offer services to optimize cloud resources for cost-efficiency, performance, and scalability.

You could also offer a package of these services or cater to businesses of different sizes, from startups to enterprises.

4. Create a Business Plan

A detailed business plan will help you map out your vision, goals, and strategies for growth. Your plan should include:

- **Market Analysis:** Understand the demand for cloud computing services in your target industries and geographical regions.

- **Revenue Model:** Decide how you'll charge clients (hourly, project-based, subscription-based for managed services, etc.).

- **Marketing Strategy:** Identify how you will attract clients. Digital marketing, networking, content creation (e.g., blogs, webinars, case studies), and SEO will be key for attracting leads.

5. Set Up Legal & Operational Framework

Ensure that your cloud services business complies with legal and regulatory requirements. This may include:

- **Business Structure:** Choose a business structure (LLC, Corporation, etc.).

- **Contracts and SLAs:** Prepare contracts and Service Level Agreements (SLAs) that clearly outline your responsibilities, expectations, and pricing.

- **Insurance and Data Compliance:** Depending on your target industry, ensure compliance with data protection laws (e.g., GDPR, HIPAA) and consider cyber liability insurance.

6. Leverage Cloud Provider Platforms

Cloud providers such as AWS, Microsoft Azure, and Google Cloud offer various programs and support for cloud consultants and service providers. Partnering with them can:

- **Increase Credibility:** Being recognized as a partner of major cloud providers can boost client confidence.

- **Access Tools and Resources:** Take advantage of free or discounted tools, technical resources, and cloud credits that can reduce costs and enhance service offerings.

7. Develop a Strong Online Presence

Establish an online presence to build credibility and attract clients. This might include:

- **Website:** Build a professional website showcasing your expertise, services, case studies, and customer testimonials.

- **Social Media:** Regularly post content on platforms like LinkedIn, Twitter, and YouTube to share thought leadership in cloud computing, industry trends, and your services.

- **Content Marketing:** Publish blog posts, eBooks, white papers, and webinars to educate potential clients on the benefits of the cloud and your offerings.

8. Sales and Customer Acquisition

- **Networking:** Attend industry events, conferences, and webinars where you can meet potential clients.

- **Cold Outreach:** Use targeted email campaigns, LinkedIn outreach, or even phone calls to engage potential leads.

- **Referrals:** Encourage existing clients to refer you to others. Word-of-mouth can be very powerful in this industry.

9. Offer Proof of Success

   - **Case Studies:** Showcase successful migrations or cloud-based solutions that resulted in measurable improvements for clients.

   - **Customer Testimonials:** Happy clients are one of your best marketing assets. Gather testimonials that highlight the benefits of your services.

   - **Pilot Projects:** Offer initial pilot projects or discounted trials to prove your value and gain trust from new clients.

10. Focus on Customer Support and Retention

   Cloud services are an ongoing relationship, so focus on providing excellent support. Offer regular check-ins, troubleshooting, and optimization services, and be proactive in ensuring your clients get the most out of their cloud investments.

Final Thoughts

Starting a cloud computing services business requires a blend of technical expertise, industry knowledge, and strong business acumen. By focusing on a niche, building strong partnerships, and delivering tangible value to clients, you can position your company for growth in the rapidly expanding cloud market.

Section 3. Sustainable Ventures

Chapter 29

Eco-Friendly Product Design

Starting an eco-friendly product design business is an exciting and impactful way to contribute to sustainability while building a profitable venture. Here's a step-by-step guide to help you launch a business that creates and sells sustainable, eco-friendly products, such as home goods, clothing, or beauty items:

Step 1: Define Your Vision and Mission

Why It's Important: Establishing a clear vision will guide your product design process and help you stay true to your eco-friendly principles.

- **Vision:** What do you want to achieve? For example, "To create beautiful, functional, and sustainable products that empower consumers to make environmentally conscious choices."

- **Mission:** Your mission should describe how you'll achieve your vision. For example, "We design eco-friendly products using materials that reduce environmental impact while supporting ethical manufacturing practices."
Consider which product categories align with your values and expertise—home goods (like eco-friendly furniture or kitchen items), sustainable clothing (upcycled fabrics, zero-waste fashion), or eco-conscious beauty products (organic skincare, reusable packaging).

Step 2: Research and Develop Your Product

Why It's Important: Sustainable products often require a deeper understanding of materials, supply chains, and environmental impact.

- **Sustainability and Materials:** Choose eco-friendly materials like bamboo, organic cotton, recycled plastics, or biodegradable products. Aim for minimal waste and reduced carbon footprints in your design process.

- **Product Lifecycle:** Consider the entire lifecycle of your product—from sourcing materials to production, packaging, usage, and eventual disposal or recycling.

- **Testing and Prototyping:** Once you have a product idea, create prototypes and test their functionality, durability, and sustainability. Consider getting feedback from potential customers to refine the design.

Step 3: Develop a Sustainable Supply Chain

Why It's Important: Your supply chain will play a huge role in the sustainability of your business.

- **Ethical Sourcing:** Source materials from suppliers who prioritize sustainability, fair labor practices, and eco-friendly manufacturing methods.

- **Local vs. Global:** Consider whether it's more sustainable to source materials locally or globally. Local sourcing can reduce your carbon footprint, but global sourcing might offer more eco-friendly options depending on the industry.

- **Packaging:** Choose recyclable, compostable, or reusable packaging. Avoid plastic whenever possible and explore alternatives like cardboard, glass, or plant-based materials.

Step 4: Create a Business Plan

Why It's Important: A clear business plan will help you stay on track, secure funding, and make informed decisions.

- **Executive Summary:** Describe the core idea of your business, your products, and what makes them unique.

- **Market Research:** Identify your target audience—eco-conscious consumers, ethical shoppers, or environmentally-focused communities.

- **Business Model:** Will you sell direct-to-consumer through an online store, partner with retailers, or use a subscription-based model for regular deliveries? Define your sales channels.

- **Pricing Strategy**: Sustainable products often cost more to produce, so plan your pricing strategy to balance cost, quality, and profitability.

- **Marketing Plan:** How will you reach your target audience? Social media, influencer partnerships, eco-friendly events, and sustainability-focused blogs can help get the word out.

Step 5: Brand Your Business

Why It's Important: Branding will help you stand out in a growing market of eco-conscious businesses.

- Brand Identity: Create a logo and visual style that reflects your commitment to sustainability. Use colors, fonts, and imagery that evoke nature, green living, and eco-consciousness.

- Brand Story: Tell your customers why you started your business. Highlight your commitment to the planet and the values that drive your work.

- Sustainability Certifications: Obtain certifications like Fair Trade, B Corp, or organic labeling, if applicable. These certifications can help build trust and credibility with your audience.

Step 6: Set Up an Online Store or Physical Presence

Why It's Important: A strong online presence will allow you to reach a global market of eco-conscious consumers.

- E-commerce Website: Set up a user-friendly website with E-commerce functionality. Use platforms like Shopify, Etsy, or WooCommerce to sell your products. Make sure your website emphasizes sustainability with eco-friendly themes and clear information about how your products are made.

- Social Media and Content Marketing: Use platforms like Instagram, Pinterest, and TikTok to showcase your eco-friendly products, share sustainability tips, and build a community of like-minded individuals.

- Packaging and Shipping: Consider eco-friendly shipping options such as carbon-neutral shipping services and minimal packaging to reinforce your brand's commitment to sustainability.

Step 7: Marketing and Growing Your Business

Why It's Important: Getting the word out will help you attract customers who align with your eco-friendly mission.

- Sustainability-Focused Content: Create blog posts, videos, or social media content around topics like eco-friendly living, sustainable product care, or behind-the-scenes looks at your production process.

- Influencer Partnerships: Partner with eco-conscious influencers who can help promote your products to their followers.

- **Collaborations and Partnerships:** Collaborate with other sustainable brands, charities, or environmental organizations to expand your reach.

- **Customer Reviews and Testimonials:** Encourage satisfied customers to leave reviews that emphasize the quality, sustainability, and positive impact of your products.

Step 8: Scale and Innovate

Why It's Important: Once your business is established, focus on growth and continual improvement.

- **Product Line Expansion:** As your brand grows, consider expanding your product offerings or entering new categories, always staying true to your sustainable values.

- **Sustainability Innovations:** Stay updated on new materials, technologies, and production techniques that reduce your environmental impact and enhance the sustainability of your products.

- **Customer Feedback:** Listen to your customers and make improvements based on their feedback. Sustainable businesses that engage with their communities often build loyal, long-term customer bases.

Final Thoughts

Starting an eco-friendly product design business is not just about selling products—it's about creating a positive environmental impact, offering consumers sustainable alternatives, and building a brand that stands for a better future. By focusing on quality, sustainability, and innovation, you can develop a successful business that aligns with your values while also contributing to a greener world.

Chapter 30

Green Energy Consulting

Starting a Green Energy Consulting business is a great way to capitalize on the global shift toward renewable energy while making a positive environmental impact. Here's a guide to help you get started:

1. Understand the Market and Your Niche

  - **Research the Green Energy Industry:** Stay updated on renewable energy trends, technologies, and regulations. The green energy sector includes solar, wind, geothermal, energy efficiency, battery storage, electric vehicles, and energy management systems.

  - **Identify Your Niche:** Green energy consulting can cover a broad range of services. Consider focusing on one or more areas:

    - **Residential Solutions:** Helping homeowners transition to solar panels, energy-efficient appliances, home battery storage, etc.

    - **Commercial Solutions:** Assisting businesses with sustainability initiatives, energy audits, solar installations, or renewable energy systems.

    - **Energy Efficiency:** Advising on how businesses or homes can reduce energy consumption and implement energy-saving technologies.

    - **Policy and Regulations:** Offering expertise on navigating local, state, and federal energy policies and incentives for renewables.

2. Develop Your Expertise and Credentials

  - **Education and Training:** A strong background in energy management, environmental science, engineering, or renewable energy systems will help. You can also take specific courses in renewable energy or energy efficiency, such as those offered by organizations like the U.S. Green Building Council (USGBC) or the American Council on Renewable Energy (ACORE).

  - **Certifications:** Certifications like LEED (Leadership in Energy and Environmental Design), NABCEP (North American Board of Certified Energy Practitioners) for solar energy, or energy auditor certifications can help establish credibility.

3. Create a Business Plan

- **Define Your Services:** What specific green energy consulting services will you offer? Be clear about the value you'll provide, whether it's conducting energy audits, recommending renewable energy solutions, helping with installations, or navigating government incentives.

- **Target Market:** Who are your ideal clients? Homeowners, small businesses, large corporations, government agencies, or non-profits? Understanding your target audience helps tailor your marketing and services.

- **Pricing Structure:** Will you charge by the hour, per project, or offer retainer-based services? Research the market rates in your area to ensure competitive pricing.

- **Revenue Streams**: Consider multiple revenue streams, such as consulting fees, referral commissions from energy providers, or partnerships with green tech companies for system installations.

4. Legal and Operational Setup

- **Register Your Business:** Choose a business name and register it with your state or local government. Decide whether you'll operate as a sole proprietor, LLC, or another entity.

- **Insurance:** Protect your business with professional liability insurance and general business insurance.

- **Licenses and Permits:** Depending on your location and the specific services you offer, you may need to obtain specific licenses or permits to operate as an energy consultant or installer.

- **Compliance with Regulations**: Familiarize yourself with local, state, and federal regulations regarding energy efficiency, renewable energy, and environmental laws. This can affect the advice you give and the solutions you recommend.

5. Build a Network and Partnerships

- **Connect with Industry Professionals:** Build relationships with renewable energy providers, installers, and manufacturers. They may refer clients to you or work with you on installations and projects.

- **Join Green Energy Associations:** Becoming a member of organizations like the American Solar Energy Society (ASES), Renewable Energy Buyers Alliance (REBA), or the Green Building Council will help you stay connected with industry trends and other professionals.

- **Partner with Other Consultants:** Partnering with other experts in energy management, construction, or engineering can expand the range of services you offer and build credibility.

6. Develop a Marketing Strategy

- **Build a Website:** Create a professional website that clearly explains your services, showcases case studies or testimonials, and educates potential clients on green energy options.

- **Content Marketing:** Write blog posts, create whitepapers, or record video content that explains the benefits of renewable energy, common questions about green energy solutions, and tips for energy efficiency.

- **Social Media:** Use platforms like LinkedIn, Instagram, and Facebook to engage with your target audience, share industry insights, and promote your services.

- **SEO and Local Marketing:** Optimize your website for search engines to attract organic traffic. Target local SEO so your business shows up when people search for "green energy consultants near me."

- **Networking and Referrals:** Attend green energy trade shows, conferences, and networking events. Word-of-mouth referrals and positive reviews can be powerful marketing tools.

7. Launch Your Consulting Services

- **Start Small and Scale:** Begin by offering consulting services to a handful of clients, focusing on high-quality work and building your portfolio. As you gain experience and grow your reputation, you can scale up by offering more services, expanding to new regions, or working with larger clients.

- **Provide Value Upfront:** Offer free consultations or energy audits to potential clients as a way to showcase your expertise and demonstrate the value you bring. You can provide energy efficiency recommendations or outline potential savings from solar or wind energy.

8. Offer Continued Support and Education

- **Ongoing Monitoring:** Once systems are installed, provide clients with continued support, including performance monitoring, troubleshooting, and updates on new energy-saving technologies.

- **Education:** Help clients understand how to maintain and optimize their systems, and keep them updated on new policies, incentives, or technologies that could benefit them.

9. Stay Updated on Industry Trends

   - **Continue Learning:** Green energy technologies are evolving quickly, so it's important to stay informed about new developments in energy storage, smart grid technology, and other innovations.

   - **Track Government Incentives:** Renewable energy incentives, tax credits, and rebates are key drivers for client decision-making. Keep up-to-date on the latest incentives and help your clients navigate these opportunities.

Final Thoughts

The green energy consulting market offers tremendous potential, as businesses and homeowners increasingly seek ways to reduce their carbon footprint and save on energy costs. By combining expertise in renewable energy solutions with a commitment to providing excellent customer service, you can build a successful business that benefits both your clients and the planet. Start small, build relationships, and stay agile as the industry continues to grow and evolve.

Chapter 31

Upcycled & Repurposed Goods

Starting an *Upcycled & Repurposed Goods* Business is a great way to combine sustainability with creativity. Here's a step-by-step guide to help you get started with turning waste or old materials into new products:

1. Identify Your Niche

The first step in starting an upcycled and repurposed goods business is to identify your niche. "Upcycled" can cover a broad range of products, from furniture and home décor to fashion, accessories, and even art. Consider the following:

- **Furniture:** Repurposing old furniture, giving it new life with paint, new fabrics, or different functions.

- **Fashion:** Turning old clothes, fabrics, or even discarded textiles into stylish new garments or accessories.

- **Home Décor:** Creating lamps, wall art, or kitchenware from materials like wood, metal, glass, or plastic.

- **Eco-friendly Packaging:** Designing products from recycled packaging or single-use plastics. Your niche will dictate the materials you need, the type of customers you'll attract, and how you market your products. Pick something that aligns with your skills, interests, and sustainability goals.

---

2. Source Materials

The heart of an upcycled business is finding old materials to transform into new products. Here's where the magic happens:

- **Thrift Stores & Garage Sales:** These are treasure troves of old furniture, clothes, fabrics, and household items.

- **Waste from Manufacturers:** Some industries, like fashion or furniture, may have leftover materials they're happy to donate or sell at a low cost.

- **Construction Sites:** Scrap wood, metal, and other construction materials can be repurposed into stylish furniture or décor items.

- **Landfills and Recycling Centers:** These places might offer opportunities for obtaining materials that others might see as waste.

- **Online Marketplaces:** Look for "free" or "donated" sections of Craigslist or Facebook Marketplace, where people are giving away or selling items they no longer need. Remember to ensure the materials are safe, clean, and can be easily worked with. Some materials might require additional treatments (like cleaning or refurbishing) before use.

3. Plan Your Products

Decide what specific items you'll create from the materials you've gathered. Some potential product ideas include:

- **Upcycled Furniture:** Chairs, tables, bookshelves, and cabinets, all reimagined and repainted or refinished.

- **Repurposed Fashion:** Old jeans turned into bags, shirts made from repurposed fabrics, or accessories like belts and scarves made from reworked leather or textiles.

- **Art and Décor:** Mirrors, picture frames, planters, and sculptures made from salvaged wood, metal, or glass.

- **Eco Products:** Reusable shopping bags, sustainable packaging, or zero-waste kits made from repurposed materials.
Focus on what you can do well, and consider starting with one category before branching out.

4. Create a Business Plan

A solid business plan will help guide your operations, set your goals, and keep you focused on what you want to achieve. Here's what to include:

- **Mission Statement:** Define your business's values and what you want to achieve—such as reducing waste, promoting sustainability, and providing affordable alternatives to mass-produced products.

- **Target Market:** Who are your ideal customers? Eco-conscious consumers, millennials, home decorators, or fashion enthusiasts might be good targets for your products.

- **Competitive Analysis:** Look at other businesses in the upcycled or sustainable market. How will your products stand out? What will make your brand unique?

- **Pricing Strategy:** Take into account material costs, your time, and any overhead costs. Ensure your pricing is competitive but still profitable.

- **Marketing Plan:** Outline how you'll promote your business, including social media, website, online marketplaces, and partnerships with sustainability organizations.

- **Funding:** Determine if you need funding for materials, tools, or marketing. You might seek a small business loan, crowdfunding, or consider starting small and scaling up over time.

5. Create Your Products

Once you have materials and a plan, start designing and creating your products. This is where your creativity comes into play! Keep in mind:

- **Quality & Safety:** Make sure your upcycled goods are functional, durable, and safe to use.

- **Aesthetic Appeal:** Focus on transforming waste into something beautiful. A product's visual appeal is key to attracting customers.

- **Unique Touch:** Find a way to make each piece feel special, whether through custom designs, finishes, or added details.
You may need to invest in some tools or equipment depending on your niche, like a sewing machine, paintbrushes, or woodworking tools.

6. Build Your Brand

Your brand will communicate your values, attract customers, and help set you apart from competitors. Some elements to consider:

- **Brand Name & Logo:** Choose a memorable name and logo that reflects the eco-friendly and sustainable nature of your business.

- **Storytelling:** People love to know the story behind the products they purchase. Share the inspiration behind your creations, how you source materials, and why sustainability matters to you.

- **Packaging:** Since you're in the upcycling space, consider using recycled or biodegradable packaging. Make sure it aligns with your eco-friendly brand.

7. Set Up Sales Channels

There are several ways to sell your upcycled goods:

- **Online Stores:** Platforms like Etsy, Shopify, or your own website are great for showcasing and selling your products.

- **Local Markets:** Farmers' markets, craft fairs, or eco-friendly pop-up events are great places to display your creations and meet customers.

- **Collaborations:** Partner with local boutiques or online eco-stores to sell your goods.

- **Social Media:** Use Instagram, Pinterest, or TikTok to show off your creations, connect with your audience, and promote your brand.

8. Market Your Business

To grow your upcycled goods business, you'll need to market effectively:

- **Social Media:** Instagram and Pinterest are especially effective for visually-driven businesses like upcycling. Share before-and-after photos, time-lapse videos of your process, and sustainability tips.

- **Content Marketing:** Start a blog or YouTube channel to showcase how you transform materials, give DIY tips, or talk about the environmental impact of upcycling.

- **Collaborations:** Work with influencers or eco-conscious brands to promote your products.

- **Word of Mouth:** Encourage customers to share their purchases on social media, offering discounts or incentives for referrals.

9. Scale and Diversify

As your business grows, look for opportunities to expand:

- **Expand Product Lines:** Start with one type of product (e.g., upcycled furniture) and add new categories like clothing, home décor, or accessories as your skills and demand grow.

- **Hire or Collaborate:** If you're growing fast, consider bringing in other upcyclers or hiring a marketing assistant to help you focus on production.

-

Sustainability Initiatives: Look for ways to make your business even more sustainable—consider offsetting carbon emissions, working with environmental charities, or further reducing waste.

10. Stay Passionate & Adapt

The key to long-term success in the upcycling business is a passion for sustainability and creativity. Keep experimenting, stay open to feedback, and adapt your offerings as customer preferences evolve. Sustainability is a growing trend, so keep your finger on the pulse of eco-conscious movements and continue finding innovative ways to turn waste into wonder!

Starting an upcycled and repurposed goods business is a rewarding journey that allows you to merge creativity with environmental consciousness. By following these steps and staying true to your sustainable vision, you can build a brand that not only thrives but also contributes positively to the planet.

Urban Farming & Vertical Gardens

Starting an urban farming and vertical gardens business can be a great venture, especially with growing interest in sustainability, local food sourcing, and home-based gardening. Here's a guide on how to approach starting this type of business, whether you plan to run a farm-to-table business or sell vertical garden kits.

Step 1: Market Research & Feasibility Study

Before diving into the business, conduct market research to understand the demand for urban farming and vertical gardens in your area.

- **Identify Your Target Audience**:
    - Urban dwellers interested in growing their own food.
    - Homeowners or apartment dwellers looking for space-saving gardening solutions.
    - Local restaurants or food outlets seeking fresh, locally grown produce.
    - Schools, businesses, or institutions interested in sustainable gardening solutions.

- **Analyze the Competition**:
    - Look for other urban farms, vertical garden suppliers, and gardening stores in your area.
    - Understand their pricing, product offerings, and unique selling propositions (USPs).
    - Identify gaps in the market or ways to differentiate yourself (e.g., unique plants, organic produce, DIY kits, etc.).

- **Assess Potential Locations**:
    - Urban farming can be done in both residential and commercial spaces, from rooftops to vacant lots.
    - Consider the space availability, access to water, and zoning regulations for farming within the urban environment.

Step 2: Define Your Business Model

You can approach this business in several ways. Decide on one or more models based on your market research and available resources.

Option 1: Farm-to-Table Business

- **Focus**: Grow fresh produce and sell directly to consumers or local businesses (restaurants, markets).

- **Product Offering**:
    - Fresh herbs, vegetables, fruits, or microgreens grown on-site using vertical farming or hydroponic systems.
    - Local, organic, and sustainably-grown products.

- **Revenue Streams**:
    - Subscription-based services (e.g., weekly or monthly delivery of fresh produce).
    - Selling produce at local farmers' markets.
    - Partnerships with local restaurants, cafes, or grocery stores.
    - Farm tours or educational workshops on urban farming.

Option 2: Vertical Garden Kits

- **Focus**: Offer DIY kits, tools, and supplies to customers who want to set up their own vertical gardens at home.

- **Product Offering**:
    - Pre-assembled vertical garden systems (e.g., hydroponic, aeroponic, or soil-based).
    - Planters, vertical garden towers, and accessories (watering systems, grow lights, etc.).
    - Seeds, starter plants, and fertilizers.
    - Online guides or workshops on how to use the kits effectively.

- **Revenue Streams**:
    - Selling kits online and in local stores.
    - Offering installation services for high-end systems.
    - Subscription services for regular delivery of plant seeds and gardening supplies.

Step 3: Create a Business Plan

A solid business plan will help guide your efforts and secure financing (if needed). Here's what you should include:

1. **Executive Summary**:
   - A brief overview of your business idea, mission, and goals.

2. **Market Analysis**:
   - Insights from your market research (target market, competitors, trends).

3. **Product/Service Description**:
   - Details of the products/services you will offer and how they address customer needs.

4. **Marketing & Sales Strategy**:
   - How you will attract customers (digital marketing, social media, word of mouth, etc.).
   - Local events or workshops to increase brand visibility.
   - Partnerships with local businesses or restaurants.

5. **Operations Plan**:
   - The day-to-day operations, including sourcing materials, production, and distribution.
   - Logistics for delivery if offering fresh produce.

6. **Financial Projections**:
   - Estimate startup costs (equipment, inventory, space, marketing).
   - Project revenue, expenses, and profits for the first 3–5 years.

7. **Legal Structure & Licenses**:
   - Decide on a business structure (sole proprietorship, LLC, etc.).
   - Obtain necessary licenses and permits, including those related to food production or selling.

Step 4: Secure Funding (if needed)

You may need to secure funding to cover startup costs. Here are a few options:

- **Self-funding**: Use personal savings or assets to get started.
- **Small Business Loans**: Research small business loans or grants for sustainable agriculture or eco-friendly businesses.
- **Investors**: Look for investors or crowdfunding if you have a compelling business model.

- **Grants & Competitions**: There are many government programs, nonprofits, and competitions that offer funding for green or urban farming initiatives.

Step 5: Set Up Your Operations

Depending on your chosen model, here's how to set up your business:

For Farm-to-Table:

1. **Site Selection**:
   - Find an appropriate space for farming, such as a rooftop, vacant lot, or even an indoor greenhouse.

2. **Farming Equipment**:
   - Invest in vertical farming systems, hydroponic equipment, or traditional soil-based setups.

3. **Supplies & Materials**:
   - Buy seeds, soil, fertilizers, and other materials needed for your crops.

4. **Staffing**:
   - If needed, hire staff to help with farming, harvesting, and deliveries.

6. **Distribution**:
   - Set up a system for packaging and delivering fresh produce to customers.

For Vertical Garden Kits:

1. **Product Design & Sourcing**:
   - Design or source the vertical garden systems and kits you want to sell.

2. **Manufacturing or Assembly**:
   - You can either manufacture your own kits, source ready-made kits from suppliers, or assemble parts yourself.

3. **Packaging & Shipping**:

- Ensure your kits are packaged for easy assembly and safe shipping. You may want to include instructions or guides.

4. **E-commerce Website**:
   - Set up an online store to sell your products. Use platforms like Shopify, Etsy, or your own website.

5. **Marketing**:
   - Create content that educates people on the benefits of vertical gardens and how to set them up at home.

Step 6: Launch Your Business

- **Website & Social Media**:
  - Build a website to showcase your products and services, including an online store.
  - Leverage social media platforms (Instagram, TikTok, Facebook) to promote your products. Highlight your urban farming methods, sustainability, and the benefits of growing food at home.

- **Launch Event**:
  - Consider hosting an opening event or launch party (virtual or in-person) to introduce your business to the community.
  - Offer special promotions or discounts to early customers.

Step 7: Scale & Grow

As your business picks up, you can scale by:

- **Expanding Product Line**:
  - Add new types of vertical garden kits or expand your produce offerings.

- **Partnerships**:
  - Collaborate with more restaurants, cafes, or local farmers' markets to distribute your products.

- **Sustainability**:

- Consider implementing sustainable farming practices or packaging to appeal to eco-conscious consumers.

- **Franchising or Licensing**:
  - If your business model proves successful, consider franchising or licensing your vertical garden kits to other cities or regions.

Final Thoughts

The key to success in the urban farming and vertical garden business is to build a strong brand around sustainability, quality, and community engagement. Whether you're growing fresh produce for local customers or providing the tools and kits for DIY gardeners, a commitment to eco-friendly practices and education will resonate with customers and help you stand out in a growing market.

Chapter 33

Electric Vehicle (EV) Charging Stations

Starting an Electric Vehicle (EV) Charging Stations business can be a lucrative opportunity given the growing demand for electric vehicles (EVs), the global shift towards clean energy, and the increasing need for accessible charging infrastructure. Here's a step-by-step guide to help you get started:

1. Conduct Market Research & Assess Demand

Before you invest in setting up EV charging stations, it's crucial to understand the market dynamics. This includes:

- **Current EV adoption rates** in your target region or country.

- **Projected EV growth** over the next 5-10 years.

- **Existing infrastructure:** Are there sufficient charging stations already, or is there a gap in coverage?

- **Target customers:** Understand who will be using the stations (e.g., individuals, commercial fleets, electric taxis, etc.).

- **Location analysis:** Identify high-traffic areas or regions with high EV ownership but insufficient charging infrastructure (e.g., shopping malls, parking lots, highways, etc.).

By gathering these insights, you can make informed decisions on location, pricing, and service offerings.

2. Create a Business Plan

A solid business plan is essential to guide your efforts, secure financing, and track your progress. Your plan should include:

- **Executive Summary:** Brief overview of your business and vision.

- **Business Model:** Decide on whether you will own and operate your own charging stations or partner with property owners to install chargers in exchange for a commission or rent.

- **Revenue Model:** How will you make money? Possible models include:

- **Pay-per-use:** Charging customers per session or kWh.

- **Subscription/ Membership Plans:** Monthly or annual memberships offering discounted rates.

- **Freemium Model:** Free or subsidized charging in exchange for data collection or advertising.

- **Competitive Advantage:** How will you differentiate yourself from competitors? (e.g., faster charging, better locations, superior customer service).

- **Growth Strategy:** How will you scale? Will you start with a few stations and expand, or target an underserved area with a network of stations?

- **Financing:** Calculate your startup costs (land, equipment, permits, installation) and consider funding options such as loans, grants, or investors.

3. Secure Financing

Starting an EV charging station network involves substantial investment. Potential costs include:

- **Site acquisition/lease** (if you are not partnering with property owners).

- **EV chargers:** The type of chargers (Level 2, DC fast chargers) and the number of units needed.

- **Installation:** Electrical work, permits, and utility setup.

- **Operational costs:** Maintenance, software platforms for monitoring, customer support, and network management.

Explore financing options such as:

- **Self-funding:** Personal savings or capital from friends/family.

- **Bank loans:** Traditional loans for business development.

- **Grants or incentives:** Many governments and local utilities offer grants or rebates for businesses installing EV charging stations.

- **Investor funding:** Venture capital or angel investors interested in the green energy sector.

4. Secure Permits and Comply with Regulations

The EV charging station business is subject to local, state, and federal regulations, so you need to:

- **Obtain necessary permits:** Contact local authorities to determine the permits required for installation and operation.

- **Electrical safety codes:** Ensure the installations meet safety and technical standards.

- **Accessibility:** Make sure the stations are accessible to all drivers, including those with disabilities.

- **Zoning laws:** Check if zoning laws allow the installation of charging stations at your chosen locations.

- **Environmental regulations:** Ensure compliance with any environmental impact regulations for electric utilities and energy sources.

5. Choose the Right EV Charger Technology & Installations

Selecting the right type of chargers depends on your target market. Key types include:

- **Level 1 Chargers:** Basic charging requires a standard 120V outlet. Best suited for home or slow-charging environments.

- **Level 2 Chargers:** Faster chargers (240V) suitable for residential or commercial use, with charging times of 3-8 hours.

- **DC Fast Chargers:** High-speed chargers (DC) capable of providing 80% charge in as little as 30 minutes. These are typically installed at highway locations for long-distance travel.

Consider partnering with reputable EV charger manufacturers like Tesla, ChargePoint, or Blink, as they offer reliable, high-quality products with customer support.

6. Find and Secure Locations

Location is a key factor in the success of your EV charging stations. Popular options include:

- **Public parking lots** (shopping malls, public garages, airports, etc.).

- **Commercial properties:** Partnering with businesses such as restaurants, hotels, and office buildings.

- **Highway locations:** For DC fast chargers that cater to long-distance travelers.

- **Residential areas:** Especially for Level 2 chargers or home charging services.

Ensure the location has access to sufficient electrical capacity to handle the demand.

7. Set Up Payment Systems & Network Management

EV drivers will expect a seamless experience, so setting up a reliable payment system is crucial. Options include:

- **Mobile apps:** Most stations allow customers to find charging locations and pay via an app. Platforms like ChargePoint, Tesla Supercharger, or EVgo offer user-friendly apps that integrate payment systems.

- **RFID cards:** Some stations use a card system for access and payments.

- **Subscription options:** Consider offering a membership or loyalty program.

Also, use a **network management platform** to monitor and manage charging stations in real-time. These platforms can help with diagnostics, software updates, and payment processing.

8. Marketing & Customer Acquisition

To grow your business, you need to attract users to your charging stations. Consider the following marketing strategies:

- **Digital presence:** Develop a website and engage in social media marketing to raise awareness about your stations.

- **Partner with EV manufacturers:** Work with car manufacturers like Tesla or Nissan to promote your charging stations to their customers.

- **Incentives:** Offer discounts, loyalty programs, or free charging trials to attract initial users.

- **Collaborate with local businesses:** Offer co-branded services at your charging stations, such as free Wi-Fi or restaurant discounts for customers while their cars charge.

- **Public relations:** Leverage news outlets, press releases, and industry events to publicize your new charging station network.

9. Offer Value-Added Services

Consider diversifying your offering to provide additional value to customers. Some possibilities include:

- **Convenience services:** Lounge areas, food, or coffee stations where drivers can relax while charging.

- **EV maintenance:** Offering basic EV services like tire checks or cleaning for customers while their cars charge.

- **Solar-powered chargers:** Promote sustainability by using solar power to charge EVs, which can reduce energy costs and attract environmentally conscious customers.

---

10. Monitor, Maintain, and Scale

Once your charging stations are up and running, the next step is to:

- **Monitor performance:** Regularly track usage patterns, customer satisfaction, and operational performance.

- **Maintain stations:** Schedule periodic maintenance to ensure optimal performance and minimal downtime.

- **Expand:** As your business grows, look for opportunities to expand to new locations or offer additional services to meet the increasing demand for EV infrastructure.

Final Thoughts

The EV charging station market is growing rapidly, offering entrepreneurs the chance to invest in a sustainable, future-focused business. By carefully planning, securing financing, selecting optimal locations, and offering exceptional service, you can build a successful business that caters to the increasing adoption of electric vehicles. Stay ahead of the curve by embracing innovation, keeping an eye on industry trends, and expanding your network as the EV ecosystem continues to evolve.

Chapter 34

Eco-Friendly Landscaping

Starting an eco-friendly landscaping business is a great way to combine environmental stewardship with entrepreneurship. Here's a step-by-step guide on how to get started:

1. Research and Define Your Niche

Eco-friendly landscaping can include various sustainable practices, so it's essential to define the specific services you'll offer. Some of the most common eco-friendly landscaping services include:

- **Xeriscaping:** Creating drought-tolerant landscapes using plants that require minimal water, reducing the need for irrigation.

- **Native Plant Gardens:** Designing landscapes with native plants that are adapted to the local environment, require less water, and attract local wildlife.

- **Rain Gardens & Swales:** Installing features that manage stormwater, improve drainage, and reduce runoff.

- **Organic Lawn Care:** Using natural fertilizers and pest control methods that don't rely on chemicals.

- **Composting and Mulching:** Offering services related to composting and applying mulch to improve soil health.

- **Sustainable Irrigation Systems:** Installing efficient, water-saving irrigation systems such as drip irrigation.

2. Research Local Regulations and Permits

Eco-friendly landscaping can involve specialized work, so it's important to familiarize yourself with any local regulations or permits you may need. This could include:

- **Water usage regulations** if you're working on xeriscaping projects.

- **Permits** for large-scale installations, such as rain gardens or hardscaping elements like retaining walls.

- **Licensing and business permits** for operating a landscaping business in your area.

3. Create a Business Plan

A solid business plan will outline your vision, services, target market, and operational plan. Include sections such as:

- **Market Analysis:** Research the demand for eco-friendly landscaping in your area. Is there a trend toward sustainable living? Are there homeowners or businesses interested in reducing their environmental footprint?

- **Services and Pricing:** Clearly outline the services you'll offer and your pricing structure. Consider offering different packages for services like lawn conversion to xeriscaping, garden installations, and maintenance plans.

- **Marketing Strategy:** Identify how you'll reach potential clients, such as through online advertising, social media, local community events, or partnerships with eco-friendly brands or organizations.

- **Financial Plan:** Estimate startup costs, ongoing expenses, and potential revenue. Factor in equipment, supplies, and labor costs, as well as any certifications or training required.

4. Obtain Necessary Equipment

To start an eco-friendly landscaping business, you'll need the right tools and equipment. However, focus on sustainability even here:

- **Eco-friendly Equipment:** Invest in electric or battery-powered tools to reduce your carbon footprint, such as mowers, trimmers, and leaf blowers. These tools are quieter and don't contribute to air pollution.

- **Water-Efficient Irrigation Systems:** Consider offering or installing water-efficient drip irrigation systems or smart sprinklers that reduce water usage.

- **Sustainable Materials:** When sourcing materials for your projects (such as mulch, soil, or stone), opt for sustainable, locally sourced, and organic products when possible.

5. Build Expertise and Certifications

Eco-friendly landscaping requires knowledge about sustainable practices, plant species, and efficient irrigation techniques. Building expertise can set you apart in the market:

- **Get Certified:** Look into certifications like the **Sustainable Landscapes** certification or other eco-friendly or horticultural certifications. This will give you credibility and show clients that you have the knowledge to back up your services.

- **Stay Informed:** Keep up-to-date on the latest trends in sustainable landscaping, water conservation techniques, and green technologies. Attend workshops, trade shows, and read industry publications.

6. Develop a Strong Online Presence

With sustainability gaining popularity, many customers will likely search for eco-friendly services online. Develop a website and social media presence to showcase your expertise. Consider the following:

- **Website:** Create a website with information on your services, a portfolio of past projects, testimonials, and easy contact information. Highlight your commitment to sustainability.

- **Social Media:** Use platforms like Instagram, Facebook, and Pinterest to post before-and-after photos of your projects, offer landscaping tips, and educate followers about sustainable practices.

- **Content Marketing:** Blog about topics like water conservation, sustainable gardening, or how to choose native plants for your area. This will help position you as an expert in eco-friendly landscaping.

7. Network with Like-Minded Businesses and Organizations

Partner with local environmental groups, sustainability organizations, and eco-conscious businesses to build your network and grow your client base. Consider:

- Joining local sustainability organizations or chambers of commerce.

- Partnering with businesses that share your environmental values, like organic nurseries or eco-friendly home improvement companies.

- Attending eco-friendly events, expos, and farmers' markets to introduce your services.

8. Offer Education and Consultations

Many clients may be interested in eco-friendly landscaping but unsure how to get started. Offering consultations and educational workshops can help position your business as an expert in the field. You can offer services like:

- **Site Assessments:** Assessing clients' properties to recommend sustainable solutions based on water availability, soil health, and local climate.

- **Workshops and Seminars:** Teaching clients about sustainable gardening practices, water-saving techniques, or how to convert their lawns to xeriscaping.

9. Focus on Customer Service and Retention

Sustainability is a long-term commitment, so offering ongoing maintenance services is crucial. Develop relationships with your clients and provide excellent customer service to build long-term business.

- **Maintenance Plans:** Offer regular maintenance services to ensure that eco-friendly landscapes remain healthy and sustainable.

- **Loyalty Programs or Discounts:** Provide incentives for clients who refer new customers or opt for ongoing maintenance contracts.

10. Track and Promote Your Environmental Impact

Lastly, make your environmental impact part of your brand. Track the water savings, reduction in chemical use, or other eco-friendly metrics of your projects, and highlight these successes in your marketing materials.

- **Create: before-and-after case studies** showcasing your work and its environmental benefits.

- Show how your efforts align with your clients' sustainability goals, whether through energy savings, water conservation, or reducing their carbon footprint.

11. Stay Committed to Sustainability

As your business grows, continue to prioritize sustainability in all aspects of your operations. For example:

- Choose eco-friendly packaging and materials for business operations.

- Offset carbon emissions if possible by supporting environmental organizations or planting trees.

Final Thoughts:

Starting an eco-friendly landscaping business allows you to create positive change while meeting a growing demand for sustainable practices. By combining your passion for the environment with your business acumen, you can provide valuable services that benefit both your clients and the planet.

With the right planning, a solid strategy, and a focus on sustainability, your business will not only thrive but also contribute to a more eco-conscious community.

Chapter 35

Carbon Offset Programs

Starting a business focused on carbon offset programs can be a rewarding and impactful way to help companies and individuals mitigate their carbon footprint while promoting environmental sustainability. Here's a step-by-step guide to launching a successful carbon offset business:

1. Understand the Carbon Offset Market

Before starting, it's essential to understand the market landscape:

- **What are Carbon Offsets?**

Carbon offsets are investments in projects that reduce or remove carbon dioxide from the atmosphere. This can include initiatives like reforestation, renewable energy projects, methane capture, and energy efficiency improvements.

- Market Demand:

Companies and individuals are increasingly recognizing the need to offset their carbon emissions to meet environmental, social, and governance (ESG) goals. Many countries have introduced regulations requiring carbon reduction, and businesses are becoming more transparent about their carbon footprints.

- Certifications & Standards:

Ensure the projects you invest in or partner with are certified by reputable bodies like the **Verified Carbon Standard (VCS), Gold Standard, or Climate Action Reserve** to assure credibility and transparency.

2. Develop a Business Model

Decide how your business will operate:

- Carbon Offset Provider:

You can either partner with existing offset projects or create your own by developing carbon-saving projects (like planting trees or building renewable energy systems).

Alternatively, you could act as a **broker** connecting companies and individuals with verified carbon offset projects.

- Target Market:

Who will be your primary customers? Companies looking to meet ESG goals, high-emission industries like transportation or manufacturing, or environmentally conscious individuals and families?

Revenue Model:

Your business could earn revenue by selling offsets directly to consumers and businesses, providing subscription services, or offering consulting services to help companies reduce emissions before offsetting them.

3. Partner with Green Initiatives

You'll need to build strong partnerships with sustainable projects to provide real, measurable offsets.

- Types of Projects:

- **Reforestation and Afforestation:** Trees absorb CO2, making this a popular carbon offset solution.

  - **Renewable Energy:** Solar, wind, hydroelectric, and biomass projects reduce reliance on fossil fuels.

  - **Energy Efficiency:** Projects that help businesses or communities reduce energy consumption.

  - **Methane Capture:** Landfills and agricultural projects can capture methane, a potent greenhouse gas.

- **Verify Projects:** Make sure the projects you work with are certified by an accredited body. This ensures that the carbon reductions are real, additional, and permanent.

4. Build a User-Friendly Platform

Most carbon offset businesses operate through online platforms where clients can easily calculate their emissions and purchase offsets. Here's what to consider:

- Carbon Emission Calculator:

Offer an online tool to help individuals and businesses calculate their carbon emissions. Many businesses, for example, need tools to estimate emissions from activities like travel, manufacturing, energy consumption, or logistics.

- Offset Purchase Process:

Make it simple for users to purchase the appropriate number of carbon credits to offset their emissions. You could offer packages based on typical carbon footprints (e.g., for flights, business operations, or households).

- Transparency and Tracking:

Provide certificates or proof of offset for customers, and allow them to track the impact of their contributions. This builds trust and demonstrates the effectiveness of the program.

5. Create a Marketing & Branding Strategy

To stand out in this growing market, your marketing strategy needs to focus on both education and value.

- Target Audience:

Identify businesses that need to offset their emissions, like tech companies, airlines, and logistics firms, or individuals who want to make environmentally responsible choices.

- Branding:

Position your company as an ethical, transparent, and trustworthy provider of carbon offsets. Highlight your commitment to the planet and provide clear information about how your offsets work.

- Marketing Tactics:

- Use social media and content marketing to educate your audience on the importance of carbon offsetting.

- Partner with influencers and eco-conscious brands to amplify your message.

- Offer a "**carbon footprint calculator**" on your website to attract visitors and potential customers.

6. Legal and Compliance Considerations

Ensure your business complies with all relevant regulations and certifications:

- Business Structure:

You can set up your company as an LLC, S-corp, or a social enterprise depending on your vision for the company (e.g., if you want to focus on profit or nonprofit goals).

- Environmental Certifications:

Familiarize yourself with standards such as the **ISO 14001** (Environmental Management), and ensure the carbon offsets are verified by third parties like VCS or the Gold Standard.

- Tax Considerations:

Understand any tax incentives or credits available to businesses involved in green initiatives. Some regions offer tax breaks for sustainable business operations.

7. Fund Your Business

To get started, you may need initial capital. Here are some funding sources:

- Personal Savings or Loans:

Start with your own capital or seek loans from banks or investors interested in green businesses.

- **Grants and Incentives:**

   Some governments and organizations offer grants for businesses promoting sustainability.

- **Venture Capital:**

   Green tech and sustainability-focused venture capital firms may be interested in investing in a business with the potential to scale and make a global impact.

8. Operations and Scaling

Once you've launched, focus on building operational efficiency:

- **Offset Management:**

   Develop a streamlined process for sourcing, verifying, and managing carbon offsets to meet client demands.

- **Customer Service:**

   Offer responsive customer service to help clients understand their emissions and manage their offset purchases.

- **Scaling:**

   As your business grows, expand your offerings by integrating more offset projects, improving your platform's functionality, or entering new geographical markets.

9. Monitor Impact and Report Progress

Ensure that your clients can see the tangible effects of their investments:

- **Annual Reports:**

   Provide transparent, regularly updated reports on how the funds are being used and the amount of CO_2 reduced.

- **Impact Metrics:**

   Showcase metrics like the number of trees planted, energy saved, or carbon dioxide emissions reduced, and share success stories of your offset projects.

10. Stay Engaged in the Sustainability Movement

Lastly, build a reputation as a thought leader in the sustainability sector by attending conferences, speaking at events, and publishing research or articles related to carbon offsets and climate action.

Final Thoughts

Starting a carbon offset business requires a deep understanding of environmental science, sustainable practices, and market trends, but it also presents a tremendous opportunity to have a meaningful impact on the planet. By developing a clear business plan, forging strong partnerships with credible green initiatives, and effectively marketing your services, you can create a successful and socially responsible business.

With the growing demand for carbon reduction and sustainability efforts, your business could play a crucial role in the global fight against climate change.

Chapter 36

Green Building & Design

Starting a Green Building & Design business is a rewarding venture that taps into the growing demand for sustainable construction and energy-efficient solutions. Whether you're offering consulting services, designing eco-friendly homes, or retrofitting existing buildings, there are key steps you can follow to establish a successful green building business. Here's a comprehensive guide on how to start:

1. Define Your Niche and Services

The green building industry is broad, so it's important to define your specific area of focus. Consider which services or consulting areas align with your expertise and market demand:

- **Sustainable Building Design:** Focus on designing new homes or commercial buildings with eco-friendly materials, energy-efficient systems, and low environmental impact.

- **Energy-Efficient Homes:** Specialize in helping homeowners or businesses optimize their energy usage through design, materials, and systems.

- **Retrofitting Existing Buildings:** Offer retrofitting solutions to help older buildings meet modern sustainability standards, such as improving insulation, installing energy-efficient windows, or incorporating renewable energy systems.

- **LEED Certification Consulting:** Help businesses or individuals pursue LEED (Leadership in Energy and Environmental Design) certification by guiding them through the process and ensuring compliance with green building standards.

- **Sustainable Materials Procurement:** Assist clients in sourcing eco-friendly building materials that minimize environmental impact.

2. Research Market Demand and Regulations

Before diving in, research the demand for green building services in your area. This includes understanding:

- **Local Regulations and Incentives:** Many cities and states offer tax incentives, rebates, or certifications for sustainable building practices. Learn what benefits your clients may be eligible for.

- **Industry Trends:** Stay informed on the latest trends in green building technologies, materials, and systems. Being knowledgeable about energy-efficient designs, renewable energy integration, and smart building technologies will set you apart.

- **Target Audience:** Identify your ideal clients—homeowners, architects, contractors, commercial developers, or public sector organizations. Assess their pain points related to sustainability, energy efficiency, and building codes.

3. Develop Your Skills and Credentials

To establish credibility in the green building space, you'll need a strong foundation of knowledge and certifications:

- **Green Building Certifications:** Certifications like LEED (Leadership in Energy and Environmental Design), BREEAM (Building Research Establishment Environmental Assessment Method), or Passive House certification will enhance your qualifications.

- **Energy Auditing Certification:** If offering retrofitting or energy efficiency services, becoming certified as an energy auditor can boost your credibility.

- **Sustainable Design Training:** Invest in education and training programs that focus on sustainable design principles, renewable energy systems, and energy-efficient building practices.

Building a strong portfolio of projects, even if they're small or volunteer-based, will also demonstrate your capability.

4. Create a Business Plan

A well-thought-out business plan will guide your startup and help secure funding. Key components include:

- **Business Model:** Will you focus on consulting, full-service design, or both? Define your primary revenue streams.

- **Target Market:** Clarify whether you're serving homeowners, commercial clients, developers, or government entities.

- **Marketing Strategy:** How will you attract clients? Consider both digital (website, social media, online ads) and traditional methods (networking events, trade shows, partnerships with architects or construction firms).

- **Pricing Structure:** Develop a pricing strategy based on local market rates, industry standards, and the complexity of your services.

- **Operations Plan:** Outline the day-to-day operations of your business, from client intake to project management and delivery.

5. Register Your Business and Obtain Necessary Licenses

Legal and regulatory requirements vary depending on your location. In general, you'll need to:

- **Register Your Business:** Choose a name, register with the appropriate local and state authorities, and secure necessary licenses.

- **Obtain Insurance:** Insurance for professional liability, general liability, and worker's compensation is essential.

- **Permits and Certifications:** If providing design services, you may need specific architectural or engineering licenses. If retrofitting buildings, ensure compliance with local building codes and energy regulations.

6. Build Your Network and Partnerships

Networking will play a significant role in your success. Consider forming partnerships with:

- **Architects, Engineers, and Contractors:** Collaborative relationships can help you access a steady stream of projects.

- **Suppliers of Sustainable Materials:** Build strong ties with suppliers of eco-friendly and energy-efficient materials to provide clients with the best options.

- **Energy Consultants:** Partnering with energy consultants or energy auditing firms can complement your services, particularly in retrofitting buildings.

- **Local Green Building Organizations:** Join organizations like the U.S. Green Building Council (USGBC), Passive House Institute, or local sustainable construction groups to stay connected with industry professionals and stay up-to-date on the latest practices.

7. Market Your Green Building & Design Services

Once your business is set up, it's time to market your services. Effective strategies may include:

- **Online Presence:** Create a professional website showcasing your services, past projects, and any certifications. Include client testimonials and case studies.

- **Content Marketing:** Write blogs or produce videos about sustainable building trends, energy-saving tips, and case studies. Position yourself as a thought leader in the green building space.

- **Social Media:** Leverage platforms like LinkedIn, Instagram, and Pinterest to share photos of your projects, green building tips, and client success stories.

- **Local Advertising:** Attend green building conferences, expos, and networking events. Also, consider local print or radio advertising for regional exposure.

8. Stay Compliant with Green Standards

As a green building consultant or designer, staying current with sustainable building standards is crucial. This includes:

- **Ongoing Education:** Continue learning about evolving green building codes, technologies, and energy-efficient systems.

- **Client Reporting:** Develop clear reports for your clients to demonstrate the impact of your services, such as energy savings, carbon reduction, and ROI.

- **Track Industry Certifications:** Ensure your designs and retrofits comply with sustainability standards like LEED, Energy Star, or Passive House to boost credibility.

9. Scale and Diversify Your Offerings

Once your business is up and running, you can look into scaling by expanding services or reaching new markets:

- **Training and Workshops:** Offer workshops on sustainable design practices or energy efficiency for homeowners or contractors.

- **Product Sales:** Consider selling eco-friendly building materials or energy-efficient technologies as part of your service offering.

- **Branch Out Geographically:** Once established locally, consider expanding your services to neighboring regions or even nationally.

10. Monitor, Adapt, and Innovate

The green building industry is evolving rapidly. Stay competitive by continually assessing market needs, exploring new technologies (e.g., smart homes, solar-powered designs), and adapting your services accordingly.

Starting a Green Building & Design business requires a blend of industry expertise, passion for sustainability, and entrepreneurial spirit. With careful planning and execution, you can position your company as a leader in the growing green construction market, helping clients build more sustainable and energy-efficient homes and businesses.

Chapter 37

Plastic-Free Product Line

Starting a **Plastic-Free Product Line** business is a meaningful and forward-thinking way to contribute to sustainability while tapping into a growing market. Here's a step-by-step guide to help you launch your own plastic-free product line focused on reusable packaging, bamboo-based products, or zero-waste solutions:

1. Define Your Vision and Values

- **Purpose:** Begin by clearly articulating why you want to start a plastic-free product line. Is it to reduce plastic waste, promote sustainability, or offer alternatives to conventional single-use plastics?

- **Target Audience:** Who are your ideal customers? Consider eco-conscious consumers, businesses aiming for sustainability, or individuals looking for zero-waste solutions.

- **Brand Values:** Your commitment to sustainability, ethical sourcing, and product quality should be at the core of your brand. These values will resonate with your audience and help you build brand loyalty.

2. Market Research & Product Selection

- **Identify Gaps in the Market:** Research the current plastic-free products available. Are there gaps or underserved niches in reusable packaging, bamboo-based products, or zero-waste solutions? Focus on products that meet existing demand but offer something unique.

- **Product Types:** Select the products that will form the foundation of your line. Some examples include:

    - **Reusable Packaging:** Beeswax wraps, cloth bags, reusable food storage containers.

    - **Bamboo-based Products:** Bamboo toothbrushes, cutlery, straws, or toothbrush holders.

    - **Zero-Waste Essentials:** Compostable dish scrubbers, biodegradable cleaning cloths, or refillable personal care items.

- **Competitive Advantage:** Determine what will set your products apart. Will you offer customization options, unique designs, or exceptional eco-friendly certifications?

3. Source High-Quality Materials

- **Eco-Friendly Materials:** For a plastic-free product line, it's important to source materials that align with sustainability. Look for biodegradable, compostable, or reusable materials. Bamboo, organic cotton, glass, stainless steel, and plant-based plastics are popular choices.

- **Ethical Sourcing:** Choose suppliers who are committed to sustainable practices. Look for certifications like Fair Trade, Organic, or FSC (Forest Stewardship Council) to ensure your materials are responsibly sourced.

   - **Test and Prototype:** Before committing to large-scale production, create prototypes to ensure that the materials and designs work effectively and are durable for everyday use.

4. Create a Business Plan

   - **Business Model:** Decide whether you want to sell directly to consumers (D2C) via an online store, or if you plan to partner with retailers, e-commerce platforms, or eco-friendly subscription boxes.

   - **Budget & Funding:** Create a financial plan to estimate your initial costs (product development, inventory, marketing, etc.). Consider crowdfunding, loans, or investors to raise capital, if needed.

   - **Revenue Streams:** Beyond direct sales, think about additional revenue streams such as offering wholesale pricing to businesses, partnering with environmental NGOs, or creating eco-friendly gift sets.

5. Branding & Packaging

   - **Brand Name & Logo:** Choose a brand name that reflects your sustainability ethos. Create a logo and design that aligns with your values—simple, clean, and eco-friendly.

   - **Sustainable Packaging:** Use minimal, biodegradable, or reusable packaging for your products. For example, recycled cardboard, paper tape, or compostable mailers. Avoid plastic at all costs.

   - **Storytelling:** Use your brand story to educate consumers on the environmental impact of plastic waste and how your products offer a practical solution. Transparency will help build trust.

6. Set Up Your Online Presence

   - **Website:** Build a user-friendly e-commerce website that showcases your products and values. Use platforms like Shopify or WooCommerce, which have built-in tools to manage product listings, inventory, and payments.

   - **SEO & Content Marketing:** Optimize your website for search engines to attract organic traffic. Create blog posts, infographics, or videos on topics like zero-waste living, sustainability tips, and plastic pollution.

   - **Social Media:** Build a presence on platforms like Instagram, Facebook, and Pinterest. Share behind-the-scenes content, customer stories, and eco-friendly tips. Engage with your community to foster a loyal following.

7. Find Suppliers & Manufacturers

   - **Supplier Relationships:** If you don't have the capability to produce products in-house, find reliable suppliers or manufacturers that align with your values. Ensure they adhere to ethical labor practices and environmental standards.

   - **Small-Scale Production:** If you're starting small, consider working with local artisans or manufacturers who specialize in sustainable products. This can help keep costs lower and support local economies.

   - **Quality Control:** Ensure that your products meet safety and quality standards, especially if they're used for food or personal care. Consider third-party certifications (like B Corp, EcoCert, etc.) to validate your claims.

8. Marketing & Launch

   - **Launch Campaign:** Plan a compelling launch campaign. Offer early-bird discounts, run social media giveaways, or create educational content that explains the environmental benefits of switching to plastic-free alternatives.

   - **Influencer Partnerships:** Collaborate with eco-friendly influencers or sustainability bloggers to get the word out about your product line. They can help promote your products to a wider audience.

   - **Sustainability Certifications:** Consider obtaining certifications such as plastic-free or carbon-neutral certifications to further validate your commitment to the environment.

9. Customer Engagement & Retention

   - **Loyalty Programs:** Offer discounts or rewards for repeat customers who make eco-friendly choices.

   - **Customer Feedback:** Actively seek customer feedback and use it to improve products. Transparency and responsiveness are key to building a strong relationship with your customer base.

   - **Community Engagement:** Get involved in sustainability efforts in your local community or partner with environmental organizations to amplify your impact.

10. Track Your Impact

   - **Measure Success:** Track the environmental impact of your business (e.g., amount of plastic saved, carbon footprint reduction). Share these results with your customers to show the tangible difference your products are making.

- **Expand Your Offerings:** As your business grows, continue to innovate and expand your product line. You could explore new materials, products, or markets to reach a broader audience.

Final Thought:

Launching a plastic-free product line requires a balance of business acumen, environmental consciousness, and creativity. By staying true to your values and offering high-quality, functional alternatives, you can create a brand that resonates with customers and makes a lasting impact on reducing plastic waste.

Chapter 38

Water Conservation Solutions

Starting a water conservation solutions business can be a rewarding venture, especially as the demand for sustainable practices continues to grow. People, industries, and governments are all seeking ways to reduce water consumption due to the increasing pressure on freshwater resources. Here's a step-by-step guide to help you get started:

1. Research the Market and Identify Needs

- **Understand the Problem**: Water conservation is needed in various sectors, such as residential, commercial, agricultural, and industrial. Research how different sectors use water and identify areas where significant savings can be achieved. For example, agricultural irrigation systems, water-efficient appliances, and smart technologies that monitor water usage are all growing trends.

- **Competitor Analysis:** Study existing companies in the water conservation space. Look at what products and services they offer, their pricing, and how they market their solutions. This will help you identify gaps in the market where you can innovate or offer a better solution.

2. Define Your Business Model

- **Product or Service Offering:** Determine whether you want to sell physical products (e.g., water-saving devices like low-flow faucets, rainwater harvesting systems, or smart water meters) or offer services (e.g., water usage audits, consulting, installation, or maintenance).

- **Target Market:** Define your target market, which could include homeowners, commercial property owners, municipalities, or agricultural businesses.

- **Revenue Model:** Decide how you'll make money. Will you sell products outright, offer subscription services for maintenance, or charge for consulting services? A combination of these approaches might be effective.

3. Create a Business Plan

- **Mission & Vision:** What is the purpose of your business? Create a clear mission statement that reflects your commitment to sustainability and water conservation.

- **Market Analysis:** Include details about the water conservation market, industry trends, and customer demographics.

- **Financial Plan:** Outline startup costs (product development, marketing, staff), expected revenue, pricing models, and profitability projections.

- **Marketing Strategy:** Develop a plan for how you'll promote your products or services. This could include social media campaigns, partnerships with environmental organizations, or targeted ads to environmentally conscious consumers.

4. Source or Develop Water Conservation Products

- **Develop or Source Products:** If you're offering physical products, you may need to either design and manufacture your own products or source them from established suppliers. For example, you could create your own line of eco-friendly faucets, water-saving irrigation systems, or leak detection sensors. Alternatively, you could partner with manufacturers that already produce these products.

- **Technology Integration:** Consider incorporating technology into your products. For example, smart water meters that provide real-time data on water usage, automatic irrigation controllers that adjust based on weather forecasts, or apps that track water consumption.

5. Obtain Necessary Certifications and Compliance

- **Regulations and Standards:** Ensure that your products comply with local regulations and standards for water-saving technologies. For example, in the U.S., products such as low-flow faucets must meet EPA WaterSense certification standards. This can enhance the credibility of your business and demonstrate to customers that your products meet industry standards for performance and sustainability.

   - **Environmental Certifications:** Consider obtaining environmental certifications that demonstrate your commitment to sustainability, such as LEED (Leadership in Energy and Environmental Design) or ISO 14001 (Environmental Management Systems).

6. Secure Funding

   - **Self-Funding:** If you have personal savings, you might consider funding your startup on your own.

   - **Loans and Grants:** Look for government grants or low-interest loans available for sustainable businesses or green technologies. Many governments offer financial incentives for businesses that promote environmental sustainability.

   - **Investors:** If you need more capital, consider attracting investors who are interested in supporting environmentally conscious startups. There are also venture capitalists and angel investors who specialize in green technologies.

7. Build Your Brand and Online Presence

   - **Branding:** Develop a brand identity that resonates with environmentally conscious customers. Your branding should reflect your commitment to sustainability and convey trust, innovation, and efficiency.

   - **Website and E-Commerce:** Create a professional website where customers can learn about your products or services, read about your mission, and make purchases. Include educational content like blogs, case studies, and testimonials to build credibility.

   - **Social Media**: Use platforms like Instagram, Facebook, LinkedIn, and Twitter to promote your products and engage with your target audience. Share water conservation tips, industry news, and customer success stories.

8. Launch and Market Your Business

   - **Partnerships:** Partner with local governments, businesses, and non-profit organizations that focus on sustainability. You could offer your products or services at a discount in exchange for visibility or endorsement.

   - **Advertising:** Use a mix of online and offline marketing strategies. Pay-per-click (PPC) advertising, content marketing, and influencer collaborations in the eco-conscious space can help spread awareness.

   - **Customer Education:** Educate your customers on the importance of water conservation, the cost-saving benefits of using water-saving devices, and how your products help achieve that goal.

9. Monitor Performance and Innovate

- **Customer Feedback:** Regularly gather feedback from customers to understand what works and what needs improvement. This can help you refine your products or services and address any emerging issues.

  - **Keep Innovating:** Water conservation technologies are evolving, and new solutions continue to emerge. Stay informed about advancements in the field and be open to adopting or developing new solutions to stay ahead of the competition.

10. Scale Your Business

  - **Expand Offerings:** Once your business is established, consider expanding your product line or service offerings. You might branch into related areas like wastewater treatment, greywater reuse systems, or water quality monitoring.

  - **Geographic Expansion:** After building a strong customer base locally, think about expanding your business to other regions or countries that face water scarcity.

Key Considerations:

  - **Sustainability:** Make sure that your products and business practices reflect the core values of sustainability. Use eco-friendly packaging, minimize waste, and focus on reducing the overall environmental footprint.

  - **Social Impact:** Consider how your business can contribute to water access for underserved communities or regions experiencing severe water scarcity. Corporate social responsibility (CSR) initiatives could include donations to water charities or the development of low-cost solutions for areas in need.

Final Thoughts

Starting a water conservation solutions business requires a deep understanding of the issues surrounding water use and a commitment to providing effective, sustainable solutions. By developing innovative products, offering services that help customers reduce water usage, and creating a strong brand focused on sustainability, your business can play a critical role in helping individuals and organizations conserve water and protect the planet's most valuable resource.

Section 4 Gig Economy & Freelancing

Chapter 39

Freelance Writing or Copywriting

Starting a freelance writing or copywriting business can be an exciting and rewarding endeavor, especially given the growing demand for content in today's digital world. With content consumption increasing, businesses and individuals alike are in constant need of high-quality writing for blogs, articles, websites, advertising copy, and more. Below are steps to help you get started with your freelance writing or copywriting business:

1. Identify Your Niche

While you can write about a variety of topics, it's often beneficial to specialize in a niche. This will help you stand out in a crowded market and attract clients who need your specific expertise. Some popular freelance writing niches include:

- **SEO content** (search engine-optimized articles)

- **Blogging** (lifestyle, travel, finance, etc.)

- **Copywriting** (advertising, product descriptions, sales pages)

- **Technical writing** (manuals, whitepapers, software guides)

- **Health and wellness writing**

- **Financial writing** (investment, personal finance, etc.)

Identifying a niche allows you to market yourself more effectively and charge higher rates because you are seen as an expert in that area.

2. Develop Your Writing Skills

Before you start landing clients, it's important to ensure your writing is top-notch. You can improve your skills by:

- **Practicing regularly**: Write every day, even if it's just journaling or writing short pieces.

- **Taking courses or workshops:** Consider taking online writing courses, such as those offered on platforms like Coursera, Udemy, or Skillshare.

- **Reading:** Read blogs, articles, and books in your chosen niche to understand the tone, style, and language your audience prefers.

- **Studying successful copywriting:** Copywriting, in particular, is a skill that blends creativity with persuasion. Analyze successful ad copy and learn the psychology behind it.

3. Build a Portfolio

To attract clients, you need a portfolio that showcases your work. If you don't have any paid clients yet, you can create samples in your niche to display your writing skills. Some ways to build a portfolio include:

- **Writing your own blog:** Start a blog in your niche, or even a general writing blog, to demonstrate your writing ability.

- **Offering free work:** Initially, you might work for free or at a discounted rate to build up samples, especially if you're just getting started.

- **Guest posting:** Reach out to blogs or websites in your niche and offer to write a guest post in exchange for a byline and portfolio piece.

- **Create mock advertisements:** For copywriting, consider creating mock advertisements, email campaigns, or sales pages to showcase your skills.

4. Set Your Rates

Setting rates can be challenging when starting, but it's crucial to know your worth. Here are some tips for determining your freelance writing rates:

- **Research industry standards:** Rates vary by industry, writing type, and experience level. For example, copywriting may command higher rates than general blog writing.

- **Consider your experience:** As a beginner, you might start with lower rates to attract clients, but be sure to gradually raise your rates as your experience grows.

- **Charge per word, hour, or project:** Freelance writers often charge by the word, hour, or project. For blog posts, for example, you might charge per word, while for a full website copywriting project, you might charge a flat fee.

5. Create an Online Presence

To attract clients, you need to make it easy for them to find you. Building an online presence is essential for any freelance business. Here are a few ways to establish yourself:

- **Create a professional website:** Your website should include an "About" section, a portfolio, your services, and contact information. You can use platforms like WordPress, Wix, or Squarespace to create a simple, professional site.

- **Leverage social media:** Platforms like LinkedIn, Twitter, and Instagram can help you connect with potential clients and fellow writers. Share your work, insights, and tips to demonstrate your expertise.

- **Join freelance platforms:** Sites like Upwork, Freelancer, Fiverr, or specialized writing platforms like ProBlogger or Contena can help you get started by connecting you with clients who need writers.

- **Network:** Building relationships with other professionals in your niche can help you get referrals. Networking can happen both online (via forums, Facebook groups, or LinkedIn) and offline (through local events or industry conferences).

6. Pitch to Potential Clients

Once you have a portfolio and a professional presence, it's time to start reaching out to potential clients. Cold pitching may feel intimidating, but it's an essential part of growing your business. Here's how to approach it:

- **Research your prospects:** Make sure you understand the business, their content needs, and how you can provide value.

- **Craft a compelling pitch:** Keep your pitch short and to the point. Introduce yourself, explain why you're a good fit, and provide a relevant portfolio piece that aligns with their needs.

- **Follow up:** Don't be afraid to follow up if you don't get a response initially. Clients are busy, and a polite follow-up can help you stand out.

7. Provide Excellent Customer Service

In the freelance world, your reputation is everything. To build a sustainable business, you'll need to maintain good relationships with your clients. Here's how to ensure long-term success:

- **Meet deadlines:** Clients rely on freelancers to deliver quality work on time. Never miss a deadline without communicating early.

- **Communicate effectively:** Keep clients updated on the progress of the project. If issues arise, be transparent and provide solutions.

- **Request feedback and testimonials**: After completing a project, ask your clients for feedback and testimonials that you can use to promote your services.

- **Go the extra mile:** Over-deliver when possible by offering extra value, whether it's additional content or a unique perspective that improves the work.

8. Scale Your Business

As you gain more clients and your reputation grows, you may want to scale your business. Some ways to expand include:

- **Raising your rates:** As you gain more experience and a strong portfolio, you can begin charging higher rates.

- **Outsourcing:** If you have more work than you can handle, consider outsourcing some tasks (such as research or editing) to other freelancers.

- **Diversifying services:** As your skills grow, you might branch out into other types of writing or services, such as content strategy, social media management, or email marketing.

9. Keep Learning and Evolving

The world of content marketing, SEO, and digital advertising is always changing. To remain competitive, continue learning about trends in your niche, SEO best practices, copywriting techniques, and other relevant topics. This will help you offer up-to-date services and stay ahead of the curve.

Final Thoughts

Starting a freelance writing or copywriting business can be a lucrative and flexible career path. By identifying a niche, building a strong portfolio, setting fair rates, and marketing yourself effectively, you can attract clients and establish a successful freelance business. The key is to stay consistent, provide great service, and continue learning and adapting to industry trends.

As demand for content continues to rise, the opportunities for freelance writers and copywriters will only expand, making this a promising career path for those with a passion for writing and storytelling.

Graphic Design or Illustration

Starting a graphic design or illustration business focused on offering branding, logos, and visuals for digital marketing is a fantastic idea, as there's strong demand for these services in today's visual-driven world. Here's a step-by-step guide to help you get started:

1. Define Your Niche and Services

- **Identify Your Niche:** As a graphic designer or illustrator, it's essential to decide whether you'll focus on specific industries, types of clients, or artistic styles. For example, you might specialize in logo design for tech startups, branding for small businesses, or creating illustrations for social media campaigns.

- **List Your Services:** Clearly define the services you will offer. For example:

  - Branding & Identity Design (logos, color schemes, typography)

  - Logo Design

  - Illustration (custom illustrations for marketing or packaging)

  - Web and App Design

  - Social Media Visuals & Ad Design

  - Print Design (brochures, posters, business cards)

  - Packaging Design

Having a defined set of services will help you attract the right clients and communicate your expertise clearly.

2. Build a Portfolio

- **Showcase Your Best Work:** Your portfolio will be your strongest marketing tool, so ensure it showcases your best work across different projects. Include any personal, freelance, or pro bono work if you're just starting.

- **Include Case Studies:** A case study with before-and-after examples or detailed descriptions of the process (from concept to final design) can give potential clients insight into how you approach projects.

- **Create Mock Projects:** If you don't have clients yet, create mock projects for imaginary brands or redesign existing logos and branding for well-known companies to demonstrate your skills.

3. Set Up Your Business

- **Legal Structure:** Choose a business structure that suits your goals (freelancer, sole proprietorship, LLC, etc.). Research the tax implications and any legal requirements for setting up a business in your location.

- **Register Your Business Name:** Pick a unique name that reflects your style and services. Ensure the name is available as a domain name for your website and check social media handles.

- **Open a Business Bank Account:** Keep your business finances separate from your personal finances.

- **Insurance and Contracts:** It's important to have the right insurance (e.g., liability insurance) and use contracts to protect both you and your clients. Contracts should outline deliverables, timelines, payment terms, and usage rights.

4. Create Your Online Presence

- **Build a Website:** Your website should serve as the digital home for your business. Include your portfolio, services, an "About Me" section, client testimonials, and a clear contact form. Tools like Squarespace, Wix, or WordPress are great for setting up a professional-looking website with ease.

- **Set Up Social Media Accounts:** Leverage platforms like Instagram, LinkedIn, Pinterest, and Behance to showcase your work and attract potential clients. Be sure to post consistently and engage with your audience.

- **SEO for Designers:** Optimize your website for search engines so potential clients can find you when they search for relevant terms (e.g., "freelance logo designer," "branding for small businesses," etc.).

5. Price Your Services

- **Research the Market:** Look at what other designers in your area or niche are charging for similar services. Pricing can vary widely based on experience, location, and complexity of the work.

- **Pricing Models:** You can charge by the hour, project, or retainer. Decide which model works best for your business. For example:

    - **Hourly:** Ideal for smaller projects with uncertain scope.

    - **Project-based:** Standard for most design projects like logo creation or full branding.

- **Retainer:** If you plan on offering ongoing design support (e.g., monthly social media posts, regular website updates), a retainer can provide steady income.

   - **Value-Based Pricing:** As you gain experience, consider charging based on the value your design brings to the client's business, rather than just time spent.

6. Market Your Business

   - **Networking:** Build relationships with potential clients through networking events, conferences, or local business meetups. Word-of-mouth referrals are often the best way to build a design business.

   - **Cold Emailing & Outreach:** Reach out to small businesses or startups who may need branding or design work. Tailor your email to show how your services can solve their problems.

   - **Content Marketing:** Start a blog or YouTube channel to share design tips, case studies, or behind-the-scenes content. This can position you as an expert in your field and help drive organic traffic to your website.

   - **Paid Advertising:** You can run ads on platforms like Facebook, Instagram, or Google Ads to target businesses in need of design work.

7. Build Client Relationships

   - **Excellent Customer Service:** Keep communication clear and professional. Respond promptly to emails, provide regular updates on project status, and be open to feedback.

   - **Manage Expectations:** Be realistic about timelines and deliverables. Always provide clients with realistic estimates for project completion, and inform them early if there are delays.

   - **Ask for Testimonials and Referrals:** After successfully completing a project, ask satisfied clients for testimonials or referrals to help build your credibility.

8. Handle Finances and Administration

   - **Invoicing:** Use invoicing software (like FreshBooks, QuickBooks, or Wave) to send professional invoices and track payments. Make sure to clarify payment terms upfront (e.g., 50% upfront, 50% on completion).

   - **Taxes:** Keep track of all income and expenses. You may want to hire an accountant or use accounting software to stay on top of tax filings.

9. Keep Learning and Growing

   - **Stay Current:** Design trends, tools, and techniques evolve over time, so keep learning. Attend workshops, take online courses, and subscribe to design blogs.

- Expand Your Offerings: As you gain experience, you might want to offer additional services such as website design, video production, or UI/UX design. Expanding your services can help you appeal to a broader range of clients.

10. Scale Your Business

   - Hire Freelancers or Employees: As your business grows, you may need to outsource work or hire other designers to help with larger projects.

   - Automate and Streamline: Use project management tools like Trello or Asana, and automate administrative tasks like invoicing and scheduling to save time.

By following these steps, you can build a solid foundation for your graphic design or illustration business. The key is to stay consistent, offer high-quality work, and always strive to improve your skills and marketing strategies. Over time, you'll build a reputation and grow your client base.

Chapter 41

Virtual Assistant Services

Starting a Virtual Assistant (VA) Services business can be a rewarding venture, especially with the growing demand for administrative support as businesses continue to outsource tasks to streamline operations. Here's a step-by-step guide to help you get started:

1. Define Your Niche

While the demand for virtual assistants is high, it's crucial to identify a niche or specialization. Virtual assistants can offer a wide range of services, from general administrative support to more specialized tasks like social media management, content creation, bookkeeping, customer service, or executive assistance.

- **Examples of Niches:**
  - Social Media Management
  - Email and Calendar Management
  - Bookkeeping and Invoicing
  - Customer Support
  - Data Entry and Research
  - Travel and Event Planning
  - Real Estate Assistance
  - Content Writing or Editing

Identifying a specific niche can help you stand out and attract clients who need your particular expertise.

2. Set Up Your Business Structure

Before launching your VA business, decide on the legal structure. Some common options include:

- **Sole Proprietorship:** Simple to set up, but you're personally responsible for any debts or liabilities.

- **Limited Liability Company (LLC):** Provides liability protection while offering flexibility in taxation.

- **Corporation:** Best for larger businesses, offering liability protection but more administrative requirements.

Research the legal requirements for your location (business licenses, tax ID numbers, etc.), and consider consulting with an attorney or accountant to choose the right structure for you.

3. Create a Business Plan

A clear business plan is essential for guiding your operations and attracting potential clients or investors. Your business plan should include:

- **Mission and Vision:** What problem are you solving for your clients, and what are your goals for the business?

- **Services Offered:** List all the services you'll provide, their pricing, and how you'll deliver them (remotely, through email, phone, video calls, etc.).

- **Target Market:** Define your ideal clients (small businesses, entrepreneurs, busy professionals, etc.).

- **Marketing Strategy:** How will you find clients? (e.g., networking, online advertising, content marketing, etc.).

- **Financial Projections:** Estimate your income, expenses, and profits. Consider how many clients you need to reach your financial goals.

4. Set Your Pricing

Pricing can be tricky because it depends on the services you offer, your experience, and the market rate. Research what other VAs are charging in your niche. There are generally three types of pricing models:

- **Hourly Rate:** Charging clients by the hour is the most common pricing method. Rates can vary widely depending on your niche, but they typically range from $25 to $75+ per hour.

- **Retainer:** Offer a set number of hours or tasks per month for a flat fee.

- **Package Pricing:** Bundle specific services into packages at a discounted rate.

Make sure your pricing is competitive, but also sustainable for you.

5. Set Up Your Home Office and Tools

As a virtual assistant, your home office will be your business hub. Make sure you have:

- **Reliable Internet and Technology:** A stable internet connection, a computer with the necessary software, and communication tools (e.g., Zoom, Skype).

- **Software Tools:** Depending on your niche, you may need specialized software, such as project management tools (Asana, Trello), accounting software (QuickBooks, FreshBooks), or marketing tools (Hootsuite, Canva).

- **Communication Platforms:** Ensure you have email, phone, or video chat capabilities that allow you to interact professionally with clients.

6. Market Your Services

Building a client base is key to your business success. Here are some effective strategies to attract clients:

- **Create a Professional Website:** Your website should showcase your services, experience, and client testimonials. Include a blog or resource center to demonstrate your expertise.

- **Social Media:** Leverage LinkedIn, Facebook, and Instagram to share helpful tips, engage with potential clients, and network with other VAs or business owners.

- **Networking:** Join online communities, attend virtual events, or participate in industry-specific groups to meet potential clients.

- **Freelance Platforms:** Platforms like Upwork, Fiverr, and Freelancer are a good place to start, especially when you're building your reputation.

- **Cold Outreach:** Reach out directly to small business owners, entrepreneurs, and organizations that may benefit from your services. Tailor your pitch to show how you can help them save time and focus on growing their business.

7. Build Client Relationships and Deliver Quality

The key to a successful VA business is building long-term relationships with your clients. Always strive to exceed expectations by:

- **Communicating clearly and frequently**

- **Delivering high-quality work on time**

- **Being professional and reliable**

- **Offering excellent customer service**

Happy clients are likely to refer you to others, which will help you grow your business.

8. Scale Your Business

Once you've established your VA business and have a steady stream of clients, consider scaling by:

- **Hiring Other VAs:** You can build a team of specialized VAs to handle different tasks, allowing you to take on more clients.

- **Outsourcing Tasks:** Hire contractors for specific tasks (e.g., website design, content writing) to expand your services without overloading yourself.

- **Expanding Services:** As you gain experience, consider offering additional services like advanced project management, digital marketing, or HR support.

9. Continue to Learn and Grow

Stay updated on the latest trends in virtual assistance, technology, and best practices. Consider:

- **Taking online courses** to expand your skill set.

- **Attending webinars and conferences** to stay connected with industry trends.

- **Joining VA networks and associations** to meet peers and mentors who can offer support.

By following these steps and staying committed to delivering value to your clients, you can build a thriving Virtual Assistant Services business. The key is to remain flexible, continuously improve your skill set, and maintain a strong reputation for reliability and professionalism.

Chapter 42

Social Media Management

Starting a Social Media Management business can be a lucrative and rewarding venture, especially if you're skilled at growing social media audiences. Many businesses recognize the importance of a strong online presence but don't have the time, expertise, or resources to manage their social media effectively. As a social media manager, you can help these businesses grow their brand, engage with customers, and drive sales. Here's a step-by-step guide to help you get started:

1. Assess Your Skills and Expertise

Before diving into the business side, take stock of your skills. Social media management requires:

- **Content creation:** Writing copy, designing graphics, creating videos, etc.

- **Strategic thinking:** Understanding what kind of content works best for each platform and audience.

- **Analytics:** Monitoring performance, adjusting strategies based on data.

- **Community management:** Engaging with followers, responding to comments, and fostering a loyal community.

Make sure you feel confident in your ability to handle these tasks or are willing to learn more.

2. Identify Your Niche

While it's possible to manage social media for any business, it's often helpful to specialize. A niche could be based on:

- Industry (e.g., healthcare, retail, beauty, real estate, tech, restaurants)

- Type of service (e.g., paid advertising, content creation, influencer marketing)

- Platform expertise (e.g., Instagram, LinkedIn, TikTok, Twitter)

Focusing on a niche allows you to target specific clients more effectively and can set you apart from competitors.

3. Create Your Business Plan

A well-thought-out business plan will serve as your roadmap. Consider the following key areas:

- **Services:** Define exactly what services you'll offer (e.g., social media audits, content creation, strategy development, ad management).

- **Pricing:** Decide how you'll charge—hourly, monthly retainer, or per project. Research industry rates to ensure your pricing is competitive.

- **Target Market:** Who are your ideal clients? Small businesses, eCommerce stores, or influencers? Create client personas to guide your marketing efforts.

- **Goals:** Set clear short-term and long-term goals, both for client acquisition and business growth.

4. Build Your Online Presence

To attract clients, you need to showcase your skills and expertise. Create accounts on popular social platforms (e.g., LinkedIn, Instagram, Twitter) and:

- **Develop a Portfolio:** If you don't have client work yet, create sample social media profiles or manage your own accounts to demonstrate your skills. Include metrics like engagement rates and follower growth.

- **Content Strategy:** Share valuable insights, tips, and behind-the-scenes looks at your work to engage your audience.

- **Testimonials:** Once you land a client, ask for testimonials to build trust and credibility.

5. Set Up Legal and Administrative Structures

Make sure you have the legal and financial aspects of your business in place. This includes:

- **Registering Your Business:** Depending on your location, you might need to register your business name or form a legal entity (LLC, Sole Proprietorship).

- **Tax ID:** Obtain a tax ID number from your local government.

- **Contracts:** Draft clear contracts that outline your services, pricing, timelines, and payment terms to protect both you and your clients.

- **Invoices:** Set up a system to invoice clients and keep track of payments. There are various invoicing tools available (e.g., QuickBooks, FreshBooks).

6. Find Clients

There are many ways to acquire clients for your social media management business:

- **Networking:** Attend industry events, workshops, or local business meetups to connect with potential clients. Referrals can also be a valuable source of business.

- **Cold Outreach:** Send personalized emails or messages to small business owners or brands you believe could benefit from your services.

- **Freelance Platforms:** Sites like Upwork, Fiverr, and Freelancer can help you find your first few clients. Once you build a reputation, you can transition to higher-paying, long-term clients.

- **Social Media Marketing:** Use your own social media profiles to showcase your expertise. Share client successes, case studies, and tips to attract new business.

7. Create a System for Managing Clients

As your client base grows, you'll need efficient systems in place to manage accounts, track performance, and communicate with clients. Some tools to consider:

- **Social Media Scheduling:** Tools like Hootsuite, Buffer, or Sprout Social can help you schedule posts and manage multiple accounts.

- **Analytics:** Google Analytics and platform-specific insights (e.g., Facebook Insights, Instagram Analytics) will help you measure success and optimize strategies.

- **Project Management:** Use tools like Asana, Trello, or Monday.com to track tasks, deadlines, and client feedback.

8. Keep Learning and Stay Updated

Social media trends and algorithms change frequently, so it's important to stay updated on the latest best practices. Subscribe to industry blogs, attend webinars, or take online courses to continually improve your skills.

9. Scale Your Business

Once you're successfully managing a few clients, you might consider scaling your business by:

- **Hiring a Team:** Bring on other social media managers, graphic designers, or content creators to help manage a larger client base.

- **Automation:** Use tools and workflows to automate repetitive tasks like scheduling posts and reporting, which will free up your time for more strategic work.

- **Expanding Services**: Offer additional services like paid social ads, influencer marketing, or email marketing to increase revenue.

10. Maintain Client Relationships

Building long-term relationships with clients is essential for sustaining and growing your business. Always be responsive, proactive, and transparent in your communication. Keep clients informed about campaign performance and suggest adjustments or new strategies to continue achieving their goals.

Final Thoughts

Starting a social media management business requires a mix of creativity, strategy, and business savvy. By building your skills, identifying a niche, and using the right tools, you can attract clients and grow your business over time. With dedication and consistency, you can turn your social media expertise into a thriving business.

Chapter 43

Online Tutoring or Teaching

Starting an online tutoring or teaching business can be a highly rewarding venture, whether you're teaching academic subjects or more creative disciplines like music and art. The flexibility, scalability, and growing demand for online learning make it a great choice. Here's a step-by-step guide on how to start your own online tutoring business:

Step 1: Identify Your Niche and Expertise

Before you dive into setting up your business, decide on the subjects or skills you'll teach. Your niche could be:

- **Academic subjects:** Math, Science, English, History, etc.

- **Languages:** English as a Second Language (ESL), French, Spanish, etc.

- **Test prep:** SAT, ACT, GRE, or other standardized exams.

- **Creative subjects:** Music, Art, Dance, Photography, etc.

Pick something you're passionate about and have expertise in. If you're planning to teach music, for example, you'll need proficiency in playing instruments or understanding musical theory. The clearer your niche, the easier it will be to target the right audience.

Step 2: Choose the Right Online Tutoring Platform or Tools

You can either join established online tutoring platforms or build your own platform.

1. Use Existing Platforms:

Platforms like VIPKid, iTalki, Preply, and Chegg Tutors have large user bases, providing a built-in audience for tutors. They also handle scheduling, payment processing, and marketing for you. However, they typically charge commissions (e.g., 20%–30%), and you have less control over pricing and customer acquisition.

2. Create Your Own Website:

If you prefer more control, creating your own website might be the better option. You can:

- Set your own rates.

- Have complete flexibility on teaching hours and style.

- Build a direct relationship with students.

You'll need to invest in website development, SEO, and marketing to attract clients. Platforms like Wix, WordPress, and Squarespace offer simple ways to build a professional website.

3. Leverage Video Conferencing Tools:

No matter which platform you choose, you'll need tools for communication. Most online tutors use Zoom, Skype, Google Meet, or other video conferencing software. You can also use collaborative platforms like Google Docs for shared work.

Step 3: Set Up Your Pricing Model

Decide how you will charge for your tutoring sessions. Pricing can vary widely based on:

- **Subject:** Technical subjects like math and science often command higher rates than general tutoring.

- **Experience and Expertise:** More experienced tutors can charge a premium.

- **Length of Sessions:** Decide if you'll offer short sessions (30 minutes) or longer sessions (60–90 minutes).

- **Payment structure:** You might offer hourly rates, packages of lessons, or subscriptions. Research competitive pricing in your niche to ensure you're within market expectations.

Step 4: Create a Compelling Profile and Content

Your profile is key to attracting students. Whether on a platform or your website, create a professional profile that highlights:

- **Your qualifications:** Education, certifications, teaching experience, and any relevant skills.

- **Your teaching philosophy:** Explain how you approach tutoring. For example, do you focus on active learning, practical examples, or personalized lesson plans?

- **Testimonials:** If you have previous students, ask for testimonials or reviews to showcase your success.

- **A sample lesson:** Offering a sample lesson or a free consultation can help potential students understand your teaching style and connect with you.

Step 5: Set Up Scheduling and Payment Systems

Make it easy for students to book sessions with you. Use scheduling tools like Calendly, Acuity, or even built-in booking systems on tutoring platforms. This will automate the booking process and prevent scheduling conflicts.

For payments, platforms like PayPal, Stripe, or direct bank transfers are commonly used. If you're using a tutoring platform, the platform will generally handle payments for you.

Step 6: Market Your Online Tutoring Business

Once your business is set up, you need to attract students. Consider these marketing strategies:

- **Social media:** Use platforms like Instagram, Facebook, and LinkedIn to promote your services. Share teaching tips, success stories, and content related to your subject.

- **Content marketing:** Write blog posts or create YouTube videos related to your niche to attract search traffic.

- **Referral programs:** Encourage your existing students to refer friends or family by offering a discount or bonus for every new student they bring.

- **Local advertising:** Even though you're teaching online, you can still promote your services in local communities through flyers, local Facebook groups, or word of mouth.

- **SEO:** If you're running your own website, make sure your site is optimized for search engines so people can find you when searching for tutors in your subject area.

Step 7: Offer High-Quality Lessons and Build Relationships

Your reputation will be key to the growth of your business, so focus on:

- **Providing high-quality lessons:** Tailor lessons to the specific needs of each student and ensure they are engaging and effective.

- **Building long-term relationships:** Be responsive, reliable, and offer personalized support. Happy students are more likely to become repeat customers and refer others.

Step 8: Scale Your Business

Once your tutoring business is established and you have a steady stream of students, consider ways to scale:

- **Offer group classes:** Teaching multiple students at once can increase your income while lowering the cost per student.

- **Create courses or resources:** You can create online courses, worksheets, or study guides that students can purchase, adding another revenue stream.

- **Hire other tutors:** If you're overwhelmed with demand, consider hiring additional tutors and offering them a commission for the students they bring in.

Additional Tips for Success

- **Stay up-to-date:** Keep improving your teaching skills and stay updated on trends in education technology or new resources that can help your students.

- **Manage your time well:** As an online tutor, time management is key. Be organized about your schedule and lesson planning.

- **Stay patient and persistent:** Building a tutoring business can take time, so be prepared for a slow start and be persistent in marketing and offering high-quality lessons.

By combining a clear niche, high-quality teaching, and strategic marketing, you can build a successful and sustainable online tutoring business that helps students achieve their learning goals while offering you a rewarding career path.

Chapter 44

Website Development

Starting a website development business can be a lucrative and rewarding venture, especially with the rise of online businesses and the ever-growing need for digital presence. Here's a guide to help you get started:

1. Develop Your Skills and Expertise

Before you begin, it's crucial to have a strong foundation in web development. This includes:

- **Front-end development:** HTML, CSS, JavaScript, and frameworks like React or Angular.

- **Back-end development:** Languages like Python, PHP, Ruby, or JavaScript (Node.js), and working with databases like MySQL, MongoDB, or PostgreSQL.

- **Full-stack development:** If you can work on both the front-end and back-end, you'll have a more well-rounded skill set.

- **Web design:** Familiarity with design tools (like Adobe XD, Figma, or Sketch) and user experience (UX) principles will be valuable.

- **Website maintenance:** Knowledge of content management systems (CMS) like WordPress or Shopify, or custom CMS development.

Stay up-to-date with the latest trends, tools, and technologies in the field to maintain a competitive edge.

2. Build a Portfolio

A strong portfolio is essential to showcase your skills and attract clients. Start by building your own website or offering to build websites for friends, family, or local businesses for free or at a discounted rate in exchange for testimonials and referrals.

- Include a variety of projects that highlight your skills: e-commerce sites, landing pages, blogs, corporate websites, etc.

- Ensure the portfolio is clean, functional, and visually appealing.

- Add case studies that detail the challenges you faced, how you solved them, and the impact of your work.

3. Create a Business Plan

A solid business plan will outline how you intend to run and grow your website development business. Key elements of your plan should include:

- **Target market:** Who are your ideal clients? Are you focusing on small businesses, e-commerce stores, non-profits, or larger corporations?

- **Services offered:** Will you specialize in custom-built websites, template customization, website maintenance, or additional services like SEO, content writing, or hosting?

- **Pricing strategy:** Decide whether you will charge hourly rates or fixed project prices. Research competitor pricing to ensure your rates are competitive.

- **Marketing and sales strategy:** How will you attract clients? Will you rely on word-of-mouth, referrals, paid ads, content marketing, or networking?

- **Operational details:** Consider what tools you need for project management, client communication, invoicing, etc. Tools like Asana, Trello, and QuickBooks may be useful.

4. Register Your Business

In most countries, you'll need to legally register your business. Choose a business name and check for domain name availability (you'll need a matching domain for your website). Depending on your location, you may need to:

- Register your business as a sole proprietorship, LLC, or corporation.

- Apply for an EIN (Employer Identification Number) if you're in the U.S. for tax purposes.

- Set up a business bank account to keep personal and business finances separate.

5. Set Up Your Online Presence

Since you're in the web development business, it's important to have a professional online presence:

- **Create your website:** Use your own skills to develop a website that showcases your services, portfolio, and contact information. Optimize it for search engines (SEO) to improve your visibility.

- **Social media profiles:** Set up professional profiles on LinkedIn, Twitter, and Instagram. Share your work, industry news, and useful resources to engage with potential clients.

- **Blog or resources:** Consider creating a blog or resources page with helpful content for business owners, like how to choose a web developer or the benefits of responsive web design.

6. Network and Market Your Services

Building relationships is key to growing your business. Networking can help you find new clients and partnerships. Consider:

- **Cold outreach:** Reach out to small businesses or entrepreneurs who might need a new website.

- **Networking events:** Attend local or online business networking events, tech conferences, or meetups.

- **Referrals and testimonials:** Ask satisfied clients for referrals or testimonials, which can help establish your reputation.

- **Online advertising:** Consider using Google Ads or social media ads to reach potential clients.

7. Pricing and Contracting

Establish clear pricing models and contract terms. Being transparent with clients about your rates, timelines, and deliverables is essential.

- **Hourly rate:** You can charge by the hour for smaller projects, ongoing maintenance, or consulting.

- **Fixed price:** For larger, more defined projects, set a fixed price based on the scope of work.

- **Payment schedule:** Typically, web development contracts have a deposit upfront, with the remainder due upon completion or at specific project milestones.

Use contracts to set clear expectations, including timelines, deliverables, and any maintenance or support services.

8. Offer Ongoing Services

One way to grow your business and build long-term relationships with clients is by offering ongoing services like:

- **Website maintenance:** Offering a monthly maintenance package that includes updates, backups, and security checks.

- **Search Engine Optimization (SEO):** Help clients improve their search engine rankings with ongoing SEO services.

- **Content updates:** Regular content additions or modifications to keep the site fresh.

- **Hosting services:** If you're technically inclined, you could offer website hosting or recommend hosting partners.

9. Focus on Customer Service

To build a sustainable business, delivering excellent customer service is essential:

- Communicate clearly and regularly with clients about project progress.

- Be responsive to questions or issues that arise after the website is launched.

- Ensure that your clients feel valued, and always ask for feedback to improve your services.

10. Scale Your Business

As your client base grows, you may need to expand your team or tools. Consider:

- **Hiring additional developers:** Bring on junior developers or contractors to handle larger projects.

- **Automating processes:** Use tools to automate invoicing, client communications, or project management.

- **Expanding services:** Branch out into related services like digital marketing, branding, or mobile app development to offer a full range of services to clients.

Final Thoughts

The demand for web development is high, and there's plenty of room for businesses that offer quality, affordable, and reliable services. By building a solid foundation with your skills, a clear business plan, and a strategic marketing approach, you'll be well on your way to launching a successful website development business.

Chapter 45

Influencer Marketing

Starting an influencer marketing business can be an exciting venture, especially with the growing demand for content creators to partner with brands. If you're aiming to build a personal brand on platforms like Instagram or TikTok and monetize it through brand partnerships, here's a step-by-step guide to get you started:

Step 1: Define Your Niche

To stand out and attract potential brand partners, it's important to focus on a specific niche. Your niche could be anything from fashion, beauty, and fitness to tech, gaming, or travel. Find something that you are passionate about and can consistently create content around. This will make your brand more authentic and attract brands that align with your values.

- Example Niche Ideas:

  - Beauty & skincare

  - Fitness & wellness

  - Food & drink

  - Travel & adventure

  - Tech gadgets

  - Sustainable fashion

Step 2: Choose Your Platform(s)

While Instagram and TikTok are two of the most popular platforms for influencer marketing, you may want to also consider other platforms like YouTube, Twitter, or even LinkedIn depending on your niche. For instance, TikTok is great for quick, viral content, while Instagram is known for curated visuals and stories.

- **Instagram:** Ideal for polished content like photos, stories, and Reels.

- **TikTok:** Best for short, engaging, and viral videos. Great for storytelling, humor, and creativity.

- **YouTube:** Long-form content, tutorials, and deep dives into topics.

Step 3: Create High-Quality, Engaging Content

To attract and grow your audience, you need to consistently create content that is both high-quality and engaging. Invest in a good camera or smartphone, editing tools, and make sure your content speaks to your niche audience.

- **Tips for Creating Content:**

  - Post consistently, whether that's daily or a few times a week.

  - Keep up with trends and challenges, especially on TikTok, to increase visibility.

  - Engage with your audience by responding to comments, DMs, and asking for feedback.

  - Focus on storytelling and creating content that adds value (e.g., tips, tutorials, behind-the-scenes).

Step 4: Grow Your Following

Focus on building an organic following by promoting your content and engaging with other users in your niche. Growth won't happen overnight, but with dedication and strategy, you can start gaining traction.

- **How to Grow Your Audience:**

  - Use relevant hashtags and keywords to improve discoverability.

  - Collaborate with other influencers in your niche.

  - Engage with your followers by liking, commenting, and responding to direct messages.

  - Run giveaways or contests to increase engagement and attract new followers.

  - Post at optimal times when your audience is most active (you can find this in the insights section of Instagram or TikTok).

Step 5: Build a Personal Brand

A personal brand is more than just the content you create; it's how you present yourself to the world. Your tone, aesthetics, and values all contribute to your personal brand.

- **Define Your Brand Identity:**

  - Decide on the tone of your voice (e.g., funny, serious, motivational, educational).

  - Choose a consistent color scheme and aesthetic for your posts.

  - Be authentic and transparent with your audience.

  - Share your personal story, struggles, and successes to create a deeper connection with your followers.

Step 6: Monetize Through Brand Partnerships

Once you've built an engaged following and established your personal brand, the next step is monetizing your platform through brand partnerships. Brands are looking for influencers who can promote their products or services to an audience that aligns with their target market.

- **How to Secure Brand Partnerships:**

  - **Reach Out:** Start by sending cold emails to brands that you align with. Make sure to include your media kit, which should include your follower count, engagement rates, audience demographics, and examples of past collaborations (if any).

  - **Join Influencer Marketplaces:** Platforms like Influencer.co, AspireIQ, and Upfluence help connect influencers with brands looking for partnerships.

  - **Create a Media Kit:** A professional media kit can help you pitch yourself to brands. Include:

    - A brief bio

    - Audience demographics (age, gender, location)

    - Engagement rates (likes, comments, shares)

    - Previous work examples

    - Your contact info and rates

  - **Negotiate Terms:** When you land a brand partnership, make sure you discuss the terms upfront, including the deliverables (number of posts, type of content, timeline, etc.), compensation, and any exclusivity clauses.

Step 7: Diversify Revenue Streams

While brand partnerships are a great way to monetize, it's smart to diversify your income streams to create more stability and growth.

- **Additional Ways to Monetize:**

- **Affiliate Marketing:** Promote products using unique affiliate links and earn a commission on sales.

   - **Selling Your Own Products or Services:** Consider creating and selling your own merchandise, online courses, or digital products like e-books or presets.

   - **Sponsored Posts & Stories:** Brands may pay you for one-off sponsored posts or Instagram Stories.

   - **Paid Subscriptions:** Platforms like Patreon, OnlyFans (if relevant), or YouTube Memberships offer paid subscription models where followers can support you directly for exclusive content.

Step 8: Scale Your Business

As your influencer business grows, it's important to scale your efforts. You might want to hire a team to help with content creation, social media management, or even PR.

- Tips for Scaling:

   - Automate some tasks (like scheduling posts) using tools like Later or Buffer.

   - Consider hiring a manager or agent to handle brand partnerships and negotiations.

   - Invest in high-quality production equipment (lighting, cameras, editing software) for a more professional look.

   - Expand to other platforms and diversify your content types (e.g., YouTube videos, podcasts, blogs).

Step 9: Maintain Long-Term Relationships

Influencer marketing is all about relationships, so building long-term partnerships with brands will be key to your success. Stay professional, transparent, and deliver on your promises to create lasting, fruitful relationships with the brands you work with.

Final Thoughts

Starting an influencer marketing business by building a strong personal brand on Instagram or TikTok is a journey that requires consistency, dedication, and strategic planning. Focus on your niche, create engaging content, and build authentic relationships with your audience and brands. As you grow, opportunities will arise for monetization, and you can scale your business into a full-fledged influencer marketing operation.

Chapter 46

Event Planning & Coordination

Starting an event planning and coordination business is an exciting and rewarding endeavor that allows you to showcase your creativity, organizational skills, and attention to detail. Whether you're planning corporate conferences, weddings, or virtual meetups, there is ample opportunity to serve both businesses and individuals. Here's a step-by-step guide to help you get started:

1. Identify Your Niche

Event planning is a broad field, so defining your niche is crucial. Consider focusing on specific types of events, such as:

- Corporate events (conferences, seminars, team-building events)
- Social events (weddings, birthdays, baby showers)
- Virtual events (webinars, online conferences, virtual meetups)
- Non-profit events (fundraisers, community gatherings)

By narrowing your focus, you'll be able to better target your marketing efforts and build a reputation in a specific area.

2. Research Your Market

Understand the demand for event planning services in your target market. Research local competitors to see what services they offer, pricing, and what makes them successful. Analyze your potential clients needs:

- Businesses may require event coordination for conferences, product launches, or employee engagement activities.
- Individuals may need help with personal milestones like weddings, birthdays, or anniversaries.
- Virtual events are becoming increasingly popular, so offering online event planning services might be a valuable addition.

Understand the specific needs of each segment and how you can differentiate yourself.

3. Create a Business Plan

A solid business plan will serve as your roadmap for success. Include the following:

- **Executive Summary:** Overview of your business, including your mission, goals, and services.

- **Market Analysis:** Insights into your target market, competitors, and potential demand.

- **Services Offered:** Details of the events you'll specialize in and any additional services you might provide (e.g., budgeting, vendor management, virtual event hosting).

- **Pricing Structure:** Outline how you will charge for your services (flat fee, hourly rate, or commission-based).

- **Marketing Strategy:** How you'll promote your services to attract clients (social media, networking, partnerships, etc.).

- **Financial Plan:** Budget for starting the business, projected revenue, and expenses.

A well-thought-out business plan can help secure funding if needed and provide a clear path for your business's growth.

4. Legal and Administrative Setup

Before launching, you'll need to handle some legal and administrative tasks:

- **Business Structure:** Decide whether you'll operate as a sole proprietor, partnership, LLC, or corporation. An LLC is often a good choice for liability protection.

- **Licensing & Permits:** Depending on your location, you may need a business license, and some events may require special permits (e.g., outdoor venues, alcohol permits).

- **Insurance:** Look into business insurance to protect yourself from liabilities, especially when dealing with large events.

- **Contracts:** Draft service contracts for clients that outline the scope of work, timelines, fees, and payment terms. It's advisable to work with a lawyer for this to ensure you're protected legally.

5. Build Your Brand & Online Presence

Develop a strong brand identity that reflects your services and values. Your branding should be consistent across all platforms (website, social media, business cards, etc.). Steps to take:

- **Business Name & Logo:** Choose a name that resonates with your target audience and design a professional logo.

- **Website:** Create a professional website with a portfolio of past events (even if you have to offer your services for free or at a discount initially to build your portfolio), client testimonials, and details about your services.

- **Social Media:** Use platforms like Instagram, Pinterest, and Facebook to showcase your work, share behind-the-scenes content, and engage with potential clients.

- **Content Marketing:** Create blogs or videos about event planning tips, trends, and challenges to build credibility and attract traffic to your website.

6. Network and Build Relationships

In the event planning business, networking is everything. Building strong relationships with vendors, venues, and clients can open doors to repeat business and referrals. Some networking strategies:

   - **Join industry associations:** Organizations like the Meeting Professionals International (MPI) or the Event Planners Association can help you connect with others in the field.

   - **Attend events:** Whether in-person or virtual, attending industry-related events can help you learn more and meet potential clients.

   - **Vendor Partnerships:** Build a network of trusted vendors (caterers, decorators, photographers, etc.) that you can rely on and refer to clients. Strong vendor relationships are key to successful event execution.

7. Invest in the Right Tools

To keep your business organized and running smoothly, invest in tools that will streamline your processes:

   - **Event Management Software:** Tools like Eventbrite, Cvent, or Asana can help you organize tasks, track deadlines, and manage client communications.

   - **Financial Tools:** Use accounting software like QuickBooks or FreshBooks to track income, expenses, and invoicing.

   - **Marketing Automation Tools:** Email marketing platforms like Mailchimp or social media schedulers like Buffer can help manage your marketing efforts.

8. Launch and Market Your Business

Once you're ready, launch your business! Consider hosting a grand opening event, even if it's virtual, to showcase your services and attract potential clients. Use these marketing tactics:

   - **Social Media Advertising:** Run targeted ads on platforms like Facebook and Instagram to reach your ideal audience.

   - **Referral Program:** Offer incentives for clients who refer new business to you (discounts, freebies, etc.).

   - **Collaborate with Influencers or Bloggers:** Partner with influencers or local bloggers who can help promote your services in exchange for exposure.

9. Focus on Customer Service and Continuous Improvement

Client satisfaction is crucial in the event planning industry, where word-of-mouth and referrals can significantly impact your business. Always strive to exceed expectations by:

- Communicating effectively with clients.

- Paying attention to detail to ensure seamless event execution.

- Gathering feedback after each event and using it to improve your services.

10. Scale Your Business

As your event planning business grows, you may want to expand your offerings or hire additional team members to help manage the workload. You can scale by:

- Offering new types of events or services.

- Expanding your geographic reach (virtual events can open up national or international markets).

- Hiring staff or subcontractors (assistants, other event planners, coordinators) to help with larger events.

Starting an event planning business can be challenging, but it's also incredibly fulfilling, especially as you help create memorable experiences for your clients. Focus on your niche, build strong relationships, and stay organized, and your business will be well on its way to success.

Chapter 47

Delivery and Ride-Sharing

Starting a delivery and ride-sharing business can be an exciting venture, especially as companies like Uber, Lyft, DoorDash, and Postmates continue to grow, offering flexible work opportunities for people worldwide. If you're interested in entering this market, you'll need to understand both the logistics of the business and the best practices for getting started. Below is a guide on how to start a successful delivery and ride-sharing business.

1. Research the Market

- **Study the Competition:** Start by researching companies like Uber, Lyft, DoorDash, and Postmates. Understand their business models, pricing, target customers, and service areas. This will help you identify gaps in the market that you could potentially fill.

- **Identify Your Niche:** Decide whether you want to focus on ride-sharing, food delivery, or a combination of both. Each has its own unique challenges and opportunities. You might also consider offering additional services, like package delivery or courier services, to diversify your offerings.

- **Regulatory Landscape:** Different cities and regions have different laws and regulations governing ride-sharing and delivery services. Make sure you understand these regulations and any necessary licensing requirements.

2. Create a Business Plan

- **Mission and Vision:** Define your business's purpose and long-term goals. For example, you might want to provide faster service, better customer support, or more flexible driver schedules.

- **Market Analysis:** Identify your target market. Are you focusing on college students needing rides, busy professionals ordering food, or elderly customers requiring assistance with deliveries? The more specific you are, the better you can tailor your services.

- **Revenue Model:** Decide how you'll generate revenue. Will you take a percentage of each ride or delivery, charge a flat fee, or have tiered pricing based on service level? Consider your pricing strategy carefully to stay competitive while maintaining profitability.

- **Startup Costs:** Estimate the initial capital needed to launch your business. This may include the development of a mobile app (if you're not using an existing platform), marketing, hiring drivers, vehicle maintenance, insurance, and customer service tools.

- **Growth Strategy:** How will you scale your business? Consider adding more vehicles, expanding into new geographic areas, or offering additional services over time.

3. Legal Considerations

- **Business Structure:** Choose a legal structure for your business (sole proprietorship, LLC, corporation). An LLC is a popular choice because it provides liability protection and allows for easier tax filing.

- **Insurance:** Secure the appropriate insurance policies. For ride-sharing businesses, this may include commercial auto insurance, liability coverage, and even accident insurance for your drivers. For delivery services, ensure you have coverage for goods being transported.

- **Driver Agreements:** Draft contracts for your drivers or contractors that clearly outline their responsibilities, compensation, and the rules they must follow while driving for you.

- **Licenses and Permits:** Apply for any necessary licenses or permits required in your area, such as a taxi or transport permit. Also, check for any zoning laws that could affect where your business can operate.

4. Develop Your Technology Platform

- **Mobile App Development:** Whether you're developing your own custom app or partnering with an existing platform (like Uber or DoorDash), you'll need a reliable, user-friendly mobile app for both drivers and customers. This app should have:

    - **User Registration:** For both riders and drivers.

    - **GPS and Mapping:** To track rides and deliveries in real-time.

    - **Payment Gateway:** To handle transactions securely.

    - **Ratings & Reviews:** To provide feedback mechanisms for customers and drivers.

   - **Website and Marketing Tools:** Create a website that explains your services and allows potential customers to sign up. You'll also need marketing tools to promote your business and acquire customers.

5. Recruit Drivers and Delivery Personnel

   - **Attracting Drivers:** Offer competitive compensation, incentives, and flexible work hours to attract drivers. If you're focusing on food delivery, you may want to target those who already work in the gig economy, such as people who drive for Uber or Lyft.

   - **Training and Support:** Provide initial training for your drivers and delivery personnel, especially around safety, customer service, and using the app. Set up a support system to handle driver issues and inquiries.

   - **Background Checks:** Perform background checks on all drivers to ensure they have clean driving records and no criminal history, as this will be critical for your business's reputation.

6. Market Your Business

   - **Local Marketing:** Use local SEO and online ads to get the word out about your new business. Consider offering promotions or discounts for first-time customers.

   - **Referral Program:** Encourage your customers to refer others by offering incentives like ride credits or discounts.

   - **Social Media:** Build a presence on social media platforms like Instagram, Facebook, and Twitter to engage with potential customers and drivers. Share special offers, customer testimonials, and other content that will generate interest.

   - **Collaborations:** Partner with local restaurants or businesses to offer exclusive deals or to promote your services in their locations.

7. Customer Support and Feedback

   - **Communication Channels:** Set up customer service channels (phone, email, live chat) to help customers with any issues or complaints. Excellent customer support is essential to building trust.

   - **Driver Feedback:** Regularly collect feedback from your drivers to improve their experience and maintain a high level of satisfaction.

- **Continuous Improvement:** Always be open to customer and driver suggestions and keep improving your services. This can include adding new features to your app, offering more payment options, or adjusting pricing.

8. Scale and Diversify

- **Expand Service Area:** Once you've established a solid customer base in your initial market, consider expanding into neighboring cities or regions.

- **New Services:** As you scale, look for opportunities to diversify your offerings. You could add ride-sharing for larger vehicles (like vans or SUVs), specialize in eco-friendly vehicles, or launch a delivery service for larger items or groceries.

- **Partnerships:** Explore potential partnerships with other businesses, like restaurants, retail stores, or even other transportation services, to broaden your network and increase visibility.

Final Thoughts

The ride-sharing and delivery market is growing fast, with many opportunities for new entrants. By doing your research, crafting a strong business plan, understanding the regulatory environment, and focusing on technology and customer service, you can build a successful business in this space. However, the key to long-term success is offering a unique value proposition, whether that's better service, higher-quality drivers, or more competitive prices.

Chapter 48

Pet Sitting or Dog Walking

Starting a pet sitting or dog walking business can be a rewarding and flexible way to earn income, especially in urban areas where busy pet owners need help taking care of their pets. Platforms like Rover make it easier to connect with clients and build your business. Here's a step-by-step guide to help you get started:

1. Research the Market

   - **Understand the Demand:** Urban areas often have a high concentration of busy pet owners, so there may be a significant demand for dog walking and pet sitting services.

   - **Identify Your Niche:** Do you want to specialize in certain types of pets or breeds? Will you offer additional services, like pet grooming, overnight care, or training?

   - **Check Competition:** Look at other pet sitters or dog walkers in your area. See what services they offer, how much they charge, and what makes them stand out.

2. Set Up Your Business

   - **Decide on the Structure:** You can operate as a sole proprietor, or you may want to register as an LLC for liability protection. Consult a local expert for the best option in your area.

   - **Get Insurance:** Pet sitting and dog walking involve a level of risk (e.g., a dog might run away or get injured). Consider pet sitting insurance to protect yourself and your clients.

- **Create a Pricing Structure:** Research what other professionals in your area charge for dog walking, sitting, or other services. You can offer flexible packages such as per-walk, per-day, or weekly rates.

3. Sign Up for Rover

   - **Create a Profile:** Rover is a popular platform for pet sitters and dog walkers. It connects you with pet owners who are looking for reliable care for their animals.

   - Include a professional photo of yourself with a pet, a description of your experience, and details about the services you offer.

   - Highlight any certifications or training you have in animal care, as this can set you apart.

   - Set your availability and pricing. Rover allows you to charge based on the type of service (e.g., a 30-minute walk vs. overnight care).

   - **Complete the Background Check:** Rover requires a background check to ensure you are trustworthy and reliable. This is a good selling point for pet owners looking for someone they can trust with their pets.

4. Prepare for the Job

   - **Pet Care Experience:** While prior professional experience in pet care is helpful, a love for animals and a commitment to their safety and well-being is just as important. Consider volunteering at a shelter or helping friends and family with their pets to build experience.

   - **Pet First Aid & CPR:** Take a course in pet first aid and CPR. This not only adds to your credibility but also prepares you to handle emergencies.

   - **Necessary Equipment:** Invest in leashes, waste bags, dog treats, toys, and any other items that will help you do the job effectively and safely.

5. Build Your Reputation

   - **Start Small:** When you first start, consider offering your services at a lower rate to attract clients and build a positive reputation. Ask for testimonials and reviews after your first few jobs, which can help you gain more clients.

   - **Provide Excellent Customer Service:** Communicate well with your clients, provide updates on their pets (especially for long walks or sitting), and always be punctual and professional.

   - **Social Media & Word of Mouth:** While Rover will help you find clients, social media can be a great tool for attracting more business. Consider creating an Instagram or Facebook page to showcase your work and share happy pet moments.

6. Expand Your Services

- **Offer Additional Services:** Once you've established yourself, you can expand your offerings to include services like:

  - Overnight stays for pets

  - Pet transportation (e.g., vet appointments or grooming)

  - Basic dog training or behavior modification

  - Pet grooming services (bathing, nail trimming)

- **Group Walks or Pack Walks:** If you're walking multiple dogs at a time, you can often offer discounted rates for group walks.

7. Stay Organized

- **Track Your Schedule and Payments:** Use scheduling and invoicing software to keep track of appointments and payments. Rover provides tools for this, but other apps like QuickBooks or Google Calendar can help you stay organized.

- **Consistency Is Key:** Whether you're offering daily dog walks or weekend sitting, clients appreciate a consistent routine. Stick to the schedule as much as possible.

8. Market Your Services

- **Online Presence:** Aside from Rover, you can list your business on local directories, create a website, or use social media platforms to engage with potential clients.

- **Referral Programs:** Offer discounts or free services for clients who refer others to your business.

- **Flyers and Business Cards:** In urban areas, posting flyers in pet stores, dog parks, and cafes can help you find local clients.

9. Keep Learning and Growing

- **Stay Updated:** Keep up with new pet care trends, dog behavior techniques, and customer service strategies.

- **Network:** Join pet care forums, groups, or associations to connect with others in the field and learn best practices.

By starting small, providing excellent service, and taking advantage of platforms like Rover, you can create a successful pet sitting and dog walking business in no time. With a love for animals and dedication to your clients, you can turn your passion into a thriving business!

Section 5. Investing & Passive Income*

Chapter 49

Real Estate Investment

Starting a real estate investment business can be a rewarding way to build wealth, generate passive income, and diversify your financial portfolio. There are several avenues you can explore, such as investing in rental properties, real estate crowdfunding, or Real Estate Investment Trusts (REITs). Each of these options has its own unique set of benefits and considerations, and the approach you choose will depend on your financial goals, risk tolerance, and available capital.

Here's a step-by-step guide on how to start your real estate investment business, focusing on rental properties, real estate crowdfunding, and REITs:

Step 1: Set Your Investment Goals

Before diving into any investment, it's crucial to define your goals. Ask yourself:

- What type of income are you seeking? (Active or passive)

- What is your risk tolerance? (Are you comfortable with high risk or do you prefer more stable, lower-risk options?)

- What is your time horizon? (Are you looking for long-term growth or short-term gains?)

- How much capital do you have to invest?

Answering these questions will guide you in deciding which type of real estate investment is right for you.

Step 2: Choose Your Investment Strategy

There are three main types of real estate investments to consider for generating passive income:

1. Rental Properties

Investing in rental properties is one of the most popular ways to generate passive income. This involves purchasing real estate—such as single-family homes, multi-family buildings, or commercial properties—and renting them out to tenants.

How to get started:

- **Research the market:** Study local real estate markets and identify areas with strong rental demand and good appreciation potential.

- **Financing:** Decide how you'll finance your property (mortgage, private funds, or other sources).

- **Property management:** You'll either manage the property yourself or hire a property management company to handle day-to-day operations (tenant screening, repairs, rent collection, etc.).

- **Evaluate cash flow:** Make sure the rental property can cover its costs (mortgage, taxes, insurance, maintenance) while generating a steady cash flow.

Benefits:

- Tangible assets you own.

- Potential for property appreciation over time.

- Steady, recurring income from rental payments.

Challenges:

- Requires significant upfront capital.

- Time and effort involved in property management or overseeing property managers.

- Ongoing expenses for maintenance and repairs.

2. Real Estate Crowdfunding

Real estate crowdfunding allows you to pool your money with other investors to fund a real estate project. This option enables you to invest in large-scale commercial or residential real estate projects without the need to buy a property outright.

How to get started:

- **Choose a crowdfunding platform:** Popular platforms include Fundrise, RealtyMogul, and Crowdstreet. Research each platform's fees, minimum investments, and available projects.

- **Diversify your investments:** Many crowdfunding platforms allow you to invest in multiple projects, helping you spread your risk.

- **Understand the returns:** Crowdfunding investments typically offer fixed returns or equity-based returns, but these can vary significantly depending on the project and its risks.

Benefits:

- Lower barrier to entry (some platforms require as little as $500 to $1,000 to start).
- Passive income with minimal involvement.
- Opportunity to invest in diverse real estate projects.

Challenges:

- Limited liquidity (your investment might be locked in for several years).
- Risk of project failure or poor returns.
- Not all platforms are equally regulated, so choose carefully.

3. Real Estate Investment Trusts (REITs)

REITs are companies that own, operate, or finance income-producing real estate. By investing in a REIT, you can own a piece of a diversified portfolio of real estate assets without having to manage properties yourself. REITs trade on major exchanges, just like stocks, so they offer a highly liquid investment option.

How to get started:

- **Research REITs:** You can invest in public REITs through stock exchanges or in private REITs through financial institutions. Public REITs are easier to buy and sell, while private REITs may offer higher returns but are less liquid.

- **Consider dividends:** Most REITs offer attractive dividend yields, which can provide regular passive income. Be sure to understand how the REIT generates income and how the dividends are paid out.

- **Assess the sector:** There are different types of REITs (e.g., residential, commercial, industrial, healthcare). Choose a REIT that aligns with your investment goals.

Benefits:

- High liquidity since REITs are traded on the stock market.
- Diversified portfolio of real estate assets.
- Lower initial investment compared to directly owning property.

Challenges:

- Subject to market volatility (stock market fluctuations can affect REIT performance).
- Potential for lower returns compared to direct property ownership.
- Management fees that can eat into returns.

Step 3: Secure Financing

Regardless of your chosen investment strategy, securing financing is essential. For rental properties, this may involve getting a mortgage. For real estate crowdfunding or REITs, you'll need to ensure you have sufficient capital to invest. Here are some financing options to consider:

- **Traditional bank loans** for rental properties.

- **Hard money loans** for short-term or high-risk investments.

- **Private lenders** or joint venture partnerships for crowdfunding or direct investment.

- **Self-directed IRAs** for tax-advantaged investing (for REITs or real estate crowdfunding).

Step 4: Conduct Due Diligence

Due diligence is crucial in any real estate investment. This involves thoroughly researching the property, project, or REIT you're considering. For rental properties, inspect the physical condition, evaluate the neighborhood, and understand local rental laws. For crowdfunding or REITs, review the track record of the platform or trust, the types of properties they invest in, and their financial performance.

Step 5: Build a Team of Experts

While you can invest in real estate alone, having a team of professionals can make the process easier and less risky. Consider building relationships with:

- **Real estate agents** or brokers with investment expertise.

- **Property managers** if you're investing in rental properties.

- **Accountants** familiar with real estate tax laws and deductions.

- **Lawyers** to handle contracts, leases, or partnership agreements.

Step 6: Monitor Your Investments

Real estate is a long-term game, but that doesn't mean you should set it and forget it. Regularly monitor the performance of your investments, whether it's checking the performance of your rental properties, reviewing returns from crowdfunding projects, or tracking the value of your REITs. Keep an eye on market trends, interest rates, and other economic factors that may impact your investments.

Step 7: Scale Your Business

As you gain experience and your portfolio grows, you can scale your real estate investment business. This may involve:

- Acquiring more rental properties.

- Diversifying into different types of real estate (e.g., commercial, industrial, or international properties).

- Investing in more crowdfunding projects or increasing your holdings in REITs.

- Partnering with other investors to pool resources for larger deals.

Final Thoughts

Real estate investing offers a range of opportunities to generate passive income, but it's important to understand your options and choose the strategy that best aligns with your financial goals. Whether you decide to invest in rental properties, participate in real estate crowdfunding, or invest in REITs, the key is to start small, conduct thorough research, and gradually scale up as you become more comfortable with the process.

Chapter 50

Dividend Investing

Starting a dividend investing business involves building a portfolio of dividend-paying stocks that generate regular income through dividends. It's a strategic way to invest, providing both the potential for capital appreciation and a steady stream of income. Here's how to approach starting a dividend investing business step-by-step:

1. Define Your Business Objectives

Before diving into the market, clearly outline the goals of your dividend investing business. For example:

- Are you focusing on long-term growth with income as a secondary goal?
- Are you targeting high-yield dividends for immediate cash flow?
- Are you planning to create a fund that clients can invest in to share the returns?

Your business model will influence the types of stocks you purchase and how you manage the portfolio.

2. Establish Your Legal and Business Structure

To run a formal dividend investing business, you will need to establish a legal business structure. Some options include:

- **Sole Proprietorship:** For a one-person operation where you're managing your own portfolio.
- **LLC (Limited Liability Company):** For liability protection and tax flexibility, especially if you're taking on investors or growing a large fund.
- **Corporation (C-Corp or S-Corp):** For raising capital from investors and scaling the business.

3. Open a Brokerage Account

To manage dividend investments, you'll need a brokerage account that supports dividend investing. Choose a broker that:

- Offers a broad range of dividend-paying stocks.
- Provides tools for tracking dividend yields, payout ratios, and growth.
- Supports tax-efficient investment strategies, such as dividend reinvestment (DRIP).

Some popular brokerage platforms include:

- **TD Ameritrade**
- **Fidelity**
- **Charles Schwab**
- **E TRADE**
- **Interactive Brokers**

4. Develop a Dividend Investment Strategy

To build a profitable portfolio, create a well-researched strategy:

- **Focus on Dividend Yield:** Identify companies that offer a high and stable dividend yield. A good yield range is typically between 3% and 6%, though it can vary based on the industry and market conditions.

- **Look for Dividend Growth:** Invest in companies with a history of consistent dividend growth (e.g., Dividend Aristocrats). These companies often have strong financials and a reliable income stream.

- **Diversify Across Sectors:** Diversify your investments across sectors such as utilities, consumer staples, healthcare, and REITs to reduce risk and ensure steady payouts.

- **Reinvest Dividends (DRIP):** Reinvest dividends to compound growth over time, especially if you're looking for long-term wealth accumulation.

- **Evaluate the Payout Ratio:** A payout ratio below 60% is typically considered sustainable, as it indicates the company has room for reinvestment while paying out dividends.

Other Considerations:

- Look for companies with strong cash flow, low debt, and consistent earnings.
- Evaluate the company's dividend history, frequency, and payout sustainability.

5. Conduct In-Depth Research on Dividend Stocks

Research the best dividend-paying stocks for your portfolio. Key resources include:

- **Dividend Stock Screeners:** Use stock screening tools like Morningstar, Dividend.com, and Seeking Alpha to identify stocks that meet your criteria for dividend yield, payout ratio, and growth potential.

- **Company Reports and Earnings Calls:** Review financial statements and earnings reports to assess the company's financial health.

- **Industry Analysis:** Ensure you understand the broader industry trends that affect dividend payments, such as regulation, competition, and market demand.

6. Start Small and Scale Gradually

When starting out, it's essential to start small to minimize risk while gaining experience. Begin with a diversified mix of large-cap, blue-chip stocks and gradually expand to other types of dividend-paying stocks (e.g., REITs, MLPs, or international stocks) as your portfolio grows. Some steps to follow:

- Invest in a few stocks at first, ensuring you understand each company's financials and dividend policy.

- Diversify across multiple sectors to avoid overexposure to one industry.

- Use dollar-cost averaging to minimize the impact of market volatility and smooth out your investment costs over time.

7. Track and Manage Your Portfolio

Managing a dividend investing business requires ongoing monitoring of your portfolio:

- **Track Dividends:** Keep a spreadsheet or use portfolio management tools to track dividend income, reinvestment, and tax obligations.

- **Evaluate Performance:** Regularly assess the performance of your investments, taking into account not just dividends but total return (including price appreciation).

- **Adjust as Needed:** Rebalance your portfolio based on changing market conditions or dividend cuts. You may need to replace underperforming stocks or add new investments to meet income goals.

8. Build Relationships and Attract Investors (Optional)

If you want to scale the business and raise capital from external investors, you'll need to:

- **Pitch Your Strategy:** Create a compelling business plan that outlines your investment strategy, target returns, and risk management approach.

- **Offer Transparency:** Investors will need clear reporting on performance, fees, and risk levels. Consider setting up a website or investor portal to provide updates.

- **Comply with Regulations:** Depending on the business structure, you may need to comply with SEC regulations if you're accepting external capital or managing funds on behalf of others. This might include registering as an investment advisor or setting up a fund.

9. Optimize Tax Efficiency

Dividend income is typically taxed differently than capital gains, so it's important to manage taxes efficiently:

- **Qualified Dividends:** Make sure the stocks you invest in pay qualified dividends, which are taxed at a lower rate than ordinary income.

- **Tax-Deferred Accounts:** Consider holding dividend-paying stocks in tax-advantaged accounts like IRAs, 401(k)s, or similar to defer taxes on dividends.

- **Tax Planning:** Consult with a tax professional to minimize tax liability and optimize your overall investment structure.

10. Continue to Learn and Adapt

Dividend investing is a dynamic strategy that requires constant learning:

- Stay informed about market conditions, interest rates, and industry news that could affect dividend payouts.

- Network with other dividend investors, attend webinars, or read books and research to continuously improve your investment strategy.

Final Thoughts

Starting a dividend investing business requires strategic planning, knowledge, and a disciplined approach to managing risk and building a portfolio. While the process of selecting stocks and managing dividends can be time-consuming, the rewards can be significant in terms of both steady cash flow and long-term capital appreciation. Whether you're investing for yourself or others, consistent execution and ongoing learning are key to success.

Chapter 51

Peer-to-Peer Lending

Starting a Peer-to-Peer (P2P) Lending business can be a rewarding venture, but it requires careful planning, regulatory compliance, and a strong business model. Below is a step-by-step guide to help you get started:

1. Understand the P2P Lending Model

P2P lending allows individuals or businesses to borrow money directly from other individuals or institutions, bypassing traditional financial intermediaries like banks. The platform facilitates the connection, often offering competitive interest rates to both borrowers and lenders. The general process involves:

- Borrowers applying for loans on the platform.

- Lenders (investors) review the applications and fund the loan requests.

- The platform charges fees for services and may provide a degree of loan servicing (such as collection and disbursement of payments).

2. Research the Market and Competition

Analyze existing P2P lending platforms like LendingClub, Prosper, or Funding Circle. Study their business models, the markets they serve, their fee structures, and the technology they use. This will help you identify gaps in the market, potential improvements, and areas where you could differentiate your platform.

3. Define Your Niche

Decide on the type of loans you want to offer and the target audience for your platform:

- **Consumer loans:** Personal loans for individuals.
- **Small business loans:** Loans for startups or small businesses.
- **Real estate loans:** Investment in property development or mortgages.
- **Student loans or debt consolidation:** A more niche area with specific requirements.

Having a defined niche will help you tailor your platform's features, marketing, and operational strategy.

4. Develop a Business Plan

Your business plan should outline the following:

- **Vision and mission** of the platform.
- **Revenue model** (how the platform will earn money, e.g., origination fees, servicing fees, late fees, etc.).
- **Marketing and customer acquisition strategies**.
- **Risk management and loan underwriting processes.**
- **Technology stack** (web platform, mobile apps, security infrastructure).
- **Regulatory compliance** (discussed further below).
- **Funding requirements** and projected costs.

A solid business plan will not only guide your decisions but also be crucial if you're seeking investment or loans to fund the startup.

5. Ensure Regulatory Compliance

P2P lending is highly regulated in most countries to ensure consumer protection, transparency, and financial stability. You need to:

- **Register with relevant financial authorities**. In the U.S., this could include the **Securities and Exchange Commission (SEC)** and state regulators. In other countries, there may be specific financial regulatory bodies to register with.
- **Comply with lending laws:** Understand and comply with laws around interest rates, consumer protection, and fraud prevention.

- **Data privacy and security:** Make sure you are adhering to data protection regulations (e.g., GDPR in Europe or CCPA in California) and have a robust cybersecurity plan to protect users' financial information.

- **KYC (Know Your Customer) and AML (Anti-Money Laundering):** Implement these processes to prevent fraud and ensure transparency.

6. Build a Technology Platform

The core of your P2P lending business is the technology platform, which connects borrowers and lenders. Key features to consider include:

- **Loan application and approval system:** A streamlined process for borrowers to submit loan requests.

- **Credit scoring and underwriting:** An algorithm to assess borrower creditworthiness (based on credit scores, income, debt-to-income ratio, etc.).

- **Loan management tools:** To facilitate payments, manage loan portfolios, and automate collections.

- **User dashboards:** Lenders should be able to track their investments and performance; borrowers should have access to their loan status.

- **Security and compliance features:** Integrate strong encryption, multi-factor authentication, and secure payment gateways.

Depending on your budget, you can either build a custom platform in-house or partner with technology providers who specialize in P2P lending software.

7. Establish Partnerships

You'll need several key partnerships to operate your P2P lending business:

- **Banks or payment processors:** To handle deposits, withdrawals, and transfers securely.

- **Credit rating agencies:** For evaluating borrower risk and creditworthiness.

- **Collection agencies:** To help recover delinquent loans.

- **Legal and compliance advisors:** To help navigate the complex regulatory landscape.

These relationships are crucial for ensuring smooth operations, compliance, and risk management.

8. Set Up Funding and Loan Terms

Define the terms and conditions of the loans that will be offered on your platform. Some key decisions include:

- **Interest rates:** Determine how rates will be set. Typically, rates are based on the borrower's risk profile, which is assessed through credit scoring and underwriting processes.

- **Loan sizes and terms:** Set the minimum and maximum loan amounts and repayment durations.

- **Fee structures:** Decide how fees will be charged (e.g., one-time fees, ongoing fees, late payment penalties).

- **Default and collection policies:** Outline the steps to be taken in case of loan defaults, including communication with borrowers and involvement of collection agencies.

9. Market Your Platform

To attract borrowers and lenders, you'll need an effective marketing strategy:

- **SEO and content marketing:** Optimize your website to rank well for key search terms related to P2P lending.

- **Digital advertising:** Use targeted ads (Google, Facebook, LinkedIn) to reach both borrowers and lenders.

- **Partnerships and referrals:** Leverage relationships with financial influencers, bloggers, and existing investors to promote your platform.

- **Branding and trust:** Building trust is key in financial services, so your platform must appear secure, reliable, and transparent.

10. Launch and Scale

After your platform is ready, it's time for the official launch. Consider a phased rollout:

- Start with a small, targeted group of borrowers and lenders to test the platform and gather feedback.

- Gradually scale up by adding more borrowers and lenders and expanding the geographic or vertical market you serve.

- Continuously monitor performance, analyze user behavior, and make iterative improvements to the platform.

11. Monitor and Improve

After launching, you'll need to keep a close eye on operations, financial metrics, and user experience. Regularly review:

- **Loan default rates:** Ensure you are managing risk effectively and adjusting underwriting criteria if necessary.

- **Lender satisfaction:** Are lenders getting the returns they expect? Are they happy with the platform?

- **Compliance:** Stay up to date with any changes in regulations and adjust your business practices accordingly.

12. Expand Your Offerings (Optional)

As your platform grows, you can explore additional ways to generate revenue and provide value:

- **Offer secondary market options** where lenders can sell their loan portfolios to other investors.

- **Develop auto-investment features** for lenders to automate their investments based on certain criteria (loan type, borrower profile, etc.).

- **Expand into international markets** if your platform proves successful in your initial geography.

Final Thoughts

Launching a P2P lending business is a complex process that involves understanding the financial markets, regulatory requirements, and technology infrastructure. By carefully planning each step, focusing on a user-friendly and secure platform, and ensuring compliance with relevant regulations, you can build a successful and scalable business in this growing industry.

Chapter 52

Buy & Sell Domain Names

Starting a **Buy & Sell Domain Names** business can be a lucrative venture if you approach it with the right strategy. Essentially, this business model involves purchasing domain names that you believe will increase in value over time, holding them until they're in demand, and then selling them for a profit. Here's a step-by-step guide to help you get started:

1. Understand the Domain Name Market

- **Research the Market:** Study the domain name industry to understand trends and factors that influence domain value, such as keyword popularity, length, domain extension (e.g., .com, .net, .org), and niche demand.

- **Learn About Domain Valuation:** Not all domains are worth the same. Factors like memorability, simplicity, keyword relevance, and global appeal can make a domain name valuable. Use online valuation tools and domain auction sites (e.g., GoDaddy Auctions, Sedo) to get a sense of what domains are selling for.

- **Trends to Watch:** Popular industries like tech, finance, health, and real estate can offer profitable domain opportunities. Keep an eye on emerging technologies and trending keywords.

2. Create a Budget and Business Plan

- **Set a Budget:** Decide how much you are willing to invest in domain names. A common starting point for new domain investors is $500 - $1,000 to purchase a few domains, but you can start with a smaller budget depending on the cost of domains you're targeting.

- **Business Plan:** Write a simple business plan outlining your investment strategy, your target domains (e.g., short, keyword-rich, or trendy), and your goals for buying and selling. Consider factors like market trends, holding time (how long you'll keep domains before selling), and your exit strategy.

3. Source Domains to Buy

- **Domain Registrars:** Use domain registrars like GoDaddy, Namecheap, or Google Domains to search for and purchase available domains. Look for expired or soon-to-expire domains, as these can sometimes be picked up at a lower cost.

- **Domain Auctions:** Check domain auction websites such as GoDaddy Auctions, Sedo, or Flippa for buying and selling domains. These platforms allow you to bid on domain names that have been previously registered.

- **Private Deals:** You may also negotiate directly with domain owners to acquire domains that aren't actively listed for sale. This might involve reaching out via email or using WHOIS information to contact the current domain owner.

- **Domains with Expiring Registrations:** Some domains may become available due to expired registrations. You can find lists of expired domains and grab them as soon as they're released.

4. Choose the Right Domains

- **Short & Memorable:** Short, catchy, and easy-to-remember domains tend to have more value. For example, a 3-4 letter .com domain is often highly sought after.

- **Keyword-Rich Domains:** Domains that include popular keywords related to industries, products, or services can be valuable because they are often easier to rank in search engines and attract more organic traffic.

- **Brandable Names:** Think about creating brandable domain names that are unique but still easy to remember and pronounce. Names that are generic but have high commercial potential can be highly valuable.

- **Popular Extensions:** While .com is the gold standard, other domain extensions like .net, .io, or .ai can also have value, particularly in specific industries like tech or startups.

5. Register the Domains

- Register your selected domain names through a reputable domain registrar. Be mindful of the renewal costs (usually $10-$20 per year per domain) as you'll need to hold onto these domains for potentially a long time before selling.

- Set up your domains with private registration to maintain anonymity, and ensure that your contact details are up-to-date to avoid losing the domain due to expiration.

6. Build a Portfolio

- As you buy domains, build a portfolio to increase your chances of having one or more highly valuable domains to sell. A portfolio also gives you credibility as a domain investor.

- Keep records of all your purchases, including purchase prices, registration dates, and any correspondence with buyers or sellers.

7. List Your Domains for Sale

- **Domain Marketplaces:** List your domains on popular domain selling platforms like Sedo, Flippa, or Afternic. These marketplaces attract potential buyers looking for specific types of domains.

- **Auction Sites:** You can auction off domains on platforms like GoDaddy Auctions to maximize the selling price.

- **Direct Outreach:** You can also approach potential buyers directly, especially if you have domains in niches like business, technology, or real estate that may appeal to specific companies or individuals.

- **Price Your Domains:** When pricing your domains, take into account factors like the keyword value, length, and demand in the market. You can start by looking at similar domain sales and adjust your pricing accordingly.

8. Negotiate and Sell

   - Negotiation: Be prepared to negotiate with potential buyers. Domain selling can be a back-and-forth process, and buyers may attempt to lower your price.

   - Escrow Services: Use an escrow service like Escrow.com to facilitate secure transactions. This protects both you and the buyer during the transfer process.

   - Transfer the Domain: Once the sale is finalized and payment is received, initiate the domain transfer process. Ensure that you follow the registrar's process for transferring ownership of the domain to the new owner.

9. Reinvest and Scale

   - As you start making sales, reinvest the profits into buying more domains. The more you diversify your portfolio and understand what types of domains sell well, the faster you can scale your business.

   - Continuously monitor trends and stay up to date on domain valuation to ensure you're making the best investment decisions.

10. Stay Compliant and Protect Your Investment

   - Ensure that you follow any legal regulations related to buying and selling domains, such as avoiding trademark infringement or purchasing domains that could potentially violate intellectual property rights.

   - Protect your personal information and financial transactions by using secure payment methods and domain privacy features.

Final Thoughts:

The key to a successful Buy & Sell Domain Names business is patience, market knowledge, and a good eye for valuable domains. Building a portfolio of high-quality domains and timing your sales for optimal value can lead to significant profits. Be prepared to spend time learning about domain trends, pricing strategies, and negotiation tactics to get the best results.

With persistence and strategy, your domain flipping business could become a sustainable source of income.

Chapter 53

Rent Out Property on Airbnb

Starting an Airbnb business can be a lucrative venture, especially as travel continues to rebound and people seek unique, flexible accommodations. Here's a guide on how to start renting out a property or room on Airbnb:

1. Research Your Market

Before jumping in, it's essential to do some market research. Understand the demand for short-term rentals in your area:

   - **Location:** Is your property in a desirable location? Consider proximity to tourist attractions, business districts, transportation hubs, or popular neighborhoods.

   - **Competitors:** Check other Airbnb listings in your area. What are their prices? How do they market themselves? What amenities do they offer?

   - **Seasonality:** Is there a high season for travel in your area? Understand peak travel times to maximize your earnings.

2. Understand Local Laws and Regulations

Every city or region has its own rules regarding short-term rentals. Before listing your property, make sure to:

- **Check zoning laws** to confirm that short-term rentals are allowed in your area.
- **Register your property** if required, and apply for necessary permits.
- **Understand tax obligations**, such as occupancy taxes or income reporting requirements.

3. Prepare Your Property

To stand out on Airbnb, your property should be clean, inviting, and well-equipped. Here's what you'll need:

- **Clean and Functional Space:** Make sure the property is spotless, organized, and well-maintained. This includes cleaning common areas, bedrooms, and bathrooms thoroughly.
- **Comfortable Furnishings:** Invest in comfortable beds, high-quality linens, and functional furniture. Think about what makes guests feel at home.
- **Essentials and Extras:** Stock up on essentials like toiletries, towels, and toilet paper. Extras like snacks, coffee machines, or a well-equipped kitchen can enhance guest satisfaction.
- **Safety Features:** Install smoke detectors, carbon monoxide detectors, and first-aid kits. Depending on local laws, you may need fire extinguishers or emergency exit plans.

4. Take High-Quality Photos

A picture is worth a thousand words, especially on a platform like Airbnb. Invest time in taking high-quality, well-lit photos of your property. Include:

- Clear, wide-angle shots of key rooms (bedrooms, living room, kitchen, bathrooms).
- Photos that showcase the best features of your space (views, outdoor areas, special amenities).
- A mix of wide shots and close-ups that highlight the details.

5. Create a Compelling Listing

When you're ready to list your property, make sure to create a description that stands out. Highlight your property's unique features and any amenities that set it apart:

- **Title:** Keep it clear and descriptive, emphasizing key selling points (e.g., "Cozy 2-Bedroom Apartment Near Downtown").
- **Description:** Write a detailed, yet concise, description of your property. Be transparent about what guests can expect. Include key amenities (Wi-Fi, free parking, air conditioning) and any local highlights (restaurants, parks, public transit).

- House Rules: Be clear about check-in/check-out times, smoking policies, noise levels, and pet rules.

   - Pricing: Research competitive pricing and set your rates based on demand, location, and the time of year. Airbnb has a "Smart Pricing" tool that adjusts prices based on market demand, but you can also manually adjust rates.

6. Set Up Your Airbnb Profile

Create a profile that builds trust with potential guests:

   - Host Profile: Add a photo of yourself and write a brief bio. A friendly, professional tone will make guests feel more comfortable booking with you.

   - Response Time: Respond quickly to inquiries and booking requests. Airbnb gives a "Response Rate" and "Response Time" score, which can influence how often your listing appears in search results.

   - Reviews: Encourage your guests to leave reviews. Positive reviews will build your credibility and attract more bookings.

7. Set Up Systems for Managing Bookings

Once your listing is live, you'll need to manage bookings efficiently:

   - Booking Settings: Choose between instant booking (where guests can immediately book) or request to book (where you approve requests). Set a minimum and maximum stay length.

   - Communication: Use Airbnb's messaging system to stay in touch with guests, answering questions and providing helpful information before, during, and after their stay.

   - Pricing Adjustments: Monitor your pricing regularly, especially during peak seasons or special events.

8. Create a Great Guest Experience

Happy guests are more likely to leave positive reviews and return for future stays. Provide a memorable experience by:

   - Being Available: Be responsive to any issues that arise during your guests' stay, whether it's a maintenance problem or a question about the area.

   - Personal Touches: Consider leaving a welcome note, offering local recommendations, or providing small amenities like toiletries or local snacks.

   - Cleanliness: Ensure the property is always clean and fresh for every guest. You might want to hire a cleaning service for turnover days.

9. Optimize and Scale Your Business

Once your Airbnb business is up and running, you can look for ways to optimize and grow:

- **Track Performance:** Monitor your occupancy rate, pricing, and guest feedback to see where you can improve.

- **Expand Your Portfolio:** Once you have gained experience and understand the business, you can scale by adding more properties to your Airbnb portfolio.

- **Automate:** Consider using tools and services that help automate booking, pricing, and communication.

10. Maintain a Strong Reputation

Building a great reputation is key to long-term success on Airbnb. Always:

- **Provide excellent customer service** and resolve issues promptly.

- **Ask for reviews** and feedback, and use them to continuously improve your service.

—By following these steps and offering a welcoming, professional experience, you can successfully launch a profitable Airbnb business. As the travel industry continues to grow, renting out property can be a rewarding way to generate income and provide valuable experiences for travelers.

Chapter 54

How to Start an Investment Business in Cryptocurrencies

Starting an investment business in cryptocurrencies can be a profitable venture, but it requires careful planning, risk management, and a solid understanding of the market. While the cryptocurrency market is highly volatile, with the right strategy, it can offer high returns for those who navigate it wisely. Here's a step-by-step guide to help you get started:

1. Educate Yourself About Cryptocurrencies

Before you start any investment business, it's essential to understand how cryptocurrencies work. This includes familiarizing yourself with the following:

- **Blockchain technology:** The underlying technology behind most cryptocurrencies.

- **Major cryptocurrencies:** Bitcoin, Ethereum, and other altcoins (e.g., Solana, Cardano, Polkadot).

- **Market dynamics:** How the crypto market behaves, the factors influencing prices, and the concept of market cycles.

- **Risk factors:** The volatility of cryptocurrencies, security risks (e.g., hacks and scams), and regulatory uncertainty.

Online courses, webinars, books, and trusted crypto resources (e.g., CoinDesk, Binance Academy, and the Ethereum website) are great ways to begin.

2. Choose Your Investment Strategy

You'll need to define the type of investment strategy that suits your risk tolerance and business goals:

- **Buy and hold (HODL):** Long-term investment strategy, buying coins with the intent to hold them for years as their value grows.

- **Trading:** Active buying and selling to take advantage of short- to medium-term price movements. Requires knowledge of technical analysis and market trends.

- **Staking and Yield Farming:** Involves earning rewards for holding and "staking" certain cryptocurrencies or participating in decentralized finance (DeFi) platforms.

- **ICO/IDO investments:** Investing in new cryptocurrency projects through Initial Coin Offerings (ICOs) or Initial DEX Offerings (IDOs).

3. Set Up Your Legal Structure

Determine the type of business structure you want for your cryptocurrency investment business. This could include:

- **Sole proprietorship:** Simple but with less liability protection.

- **Limited Liability Company (LLC):** Provides some personal liability protection while maintaining flexibility in tax treatment.

- **Corporation:** Suitable if you plan to scale the business and raise capital from investors.

Consult with a legal professional to choose the right structure for your business and ensure you comply with local regulations.

4. Understand Cryptocurrency Regulations

Cryptocurrency regulations vary widely depending on your country of operation. Before launching your investment business, research:

- **Taxation rules:** In many jurisdictions, cryptocurrency profits are taxable. Be aware of capital gains taxes and the reporting requirements for crypto transactions.

- **Licensing requirements:** Some countries require licenses or registrations for businesses dealing with cryptocurrencies.

- **Anti-money laundering (AML) and Know Your Customer (KYC):** Compliance with AML and KYC regulations may be necessary, especially if you're offering investment services to clients.

Seek legal advice to ensure compliance with local and international laws.

5. Select the Right Investment Platform

Choose a reliable platform for purchasing, storing, and managing your cryptocurrency investments. Popular platforms include:

- **Cryptocurrency exchanges:** Such as Coinbase, Binance, Kraken, or Gemini. These platforms allow you to buy and sell cryptocurrencies.

- **Wallets:** Hardware wallets (e.g., Ledger, Trezor) or software wallets (e.g., MetaMask, Trust Wallet) for secure storage of digital assets.

- **DeFi platforms:** For those interested in decentralized finance, platforms like Uniswap or Aave allow you to earn passive income through staking or lending.

Make sure the platform you choose has strong security features (e.g., two-factor authentication), a user-friendly interface, and sufficient liquidity.

6. Develop a Risk Management Plan

Cryptocurrency investments can be highly volatile, so managing risk is essential. Some risk management strategies include:

- **Diversification:** Spread your investments across different cryptocurrencies to reduce the impact of a single asset's price drop.

- **Stop-loss orders:** Set predefined limits to automatically sell assets if their value drops below a certain threshold.

- **Hedging:** Use options or other financial instruments to offset potential losses.

- **Regular portfolio reviews:** Monitor market conditions and adjust your portfolio periodically.

Decide how much capital you're willing to invest and how much risk you're comfortable with.

7. Develop a Business Plan

Your business plan should clearly outline:

- **Your target market:** Are you focusing on individual retail investors, institutional investors, or both?

- **Revenue model:** Will you charge a management fee, take a commission on trades, or operate as a hedge fund-style business?

- **Marketing and acquisition strategy:** How will you attract clients or investors to your platform? This could involve content marketing, paid ads, influencer partnerships, or referral programs.

- **Exit strategy:** Determine your long-term goals. Are you planning to sell your business, go public, or build a sustainable long-term investment operation?

8. Set Up Secure Storage and Safeguards

Cryptocurrencies are targets for cybercriminals. Ensure that your business implements robust security measures, including:

- **Cold storage:** Store most of your assets offline in cold wallets to protect them from hacking.

- **Multi-signature wallets:** Use multi-signature wallets where multiple private keys are required to authorize transactions.

- **Insurance:** Explore insurance options for cryptocurrency holdings, if available.

9. Build Trust with Clients

Building a reputation for reliability and transparency is essential for success in the cryptocurrency investment space. Some tips to establish trust:

- **Provide clear, transparent reporting:** Keep investors informed about performance, risks, and market conditions.

- **Offer educational resources:** Help clients understand the risks and benefits of cryptocurrency investments.

- **Customer support:** Offer accessible support through email, chat, or phone to answer any client concerns.

- **Be compliant:** Ensure your business complies with all relevant regulations and standards.

10. Market Your Business

Once your business is up and running, start marketing your services. Some effective marketing strategies for cryptocurrency investment businesses include:

- **Content marketing:** Create educational content such as blog posts, podcasts, videos, and webinars.

- **Social media:** Use platforms like Twitter, Reddit, and LinkedIn to engage with the crypto community.

- **Partnerships:** Collaborate with influencers or other businesses in the cryptocurrency space to build awareness and attract clients.

Final Thoughts

Starting a cryptocurrency investment business can be an exciting and lucrative opportunity if approached with caution and strategy. By staying informed, managing risks, ensuring compliance, and building trust with your clients, you can position yourself for long-term success in this rapidly evolving market. Remember, while cryptocurrencies offer high potential returns, the volatility and complexity of the market mean that careful, well-informed decision-making is critical to success.

Chapter 55

Create a Print-on-Demand Store

Starting a Print-on-Demand (POD) store is a great way to sell custom merchandise like t-shirts, mugs, phone cases, and more without having to manage inventory, production, or shipping. The print-on-demand model allows you to focus on creating unique designs and marketing your products while a third-party supplier handles the production and fulfillment. Here's a step-by-step guide to get you started:

1. Choose Your Niche

- **Target Audience:** Before diving into design, think about who you want to sell to. Are you creating merchandise for a specific interest group, like gamers, pet lovers, or fitness enthusiasts? A niche market can help your store stand out and attract loyal customers.

- **Unique Designs:** Consider what makes your designs unique. Will they be funny, inspirational, artistic, or personalized? Defining a style or theme will help you create a cohesive brand identity.

2. Select a Print-on-Demand Platform

There are many POD platforms that integrate with eCommerce sites, making it easy to set up a store. Some popular options include:

- **Printful:** A leading POD service with a wide range of products, good customization tools, and integration with platforms like Shopify, Etsy, and WooCommerce.

- **Printify:** Another great POD service with competitive pricing and integration options. Offers a large catalog of products and printing partners.

- **Teespring (now Spring):** Known for being beginner-friendly, Teespring lets you create a storefront and easily sell across multiple platforms.

- **Gooten:** Offers a global production network and integrates with major eCommerce platforms like Shopify and Etsy.

Tip: Look at the product catalog, pricing, and shipping options of each platform to see which fits your needs best.

3. Set Up Your Online Store

Once you've chosen a POD platform, it's time to set up your online store. Depending on the platform, this will be integrated directly into your POD provider or require using an external eCommerce platform. Here are a few options:

- **Shopify:** One of the most popular platforms for building online stores, Shopify integrates seamlessly with POD providers like Printful and Printify.

- **Etsy:** If you're targeting handmade or niche products, Etsy is a great marketplace for POD stores.

- **WooCommerce:** A plugin for WordPress sites, WooCommerce allows you to sell products directly on your website while integrating with POD services.

- **BigCommerce:** Another robust platform for setting up an online store with integration to POD services.

4. Design Your Merchandise

- **Create Your Designs:** Using design tools like Adobe Illustrator, Photoshop, Canva, or free tools like GIMP, create eye-catching designs that will look great on your products. Make sure to consider how your designs will fit the different products you're offering (e.g., t-shirts, mugs, phone cases).

  - For t-shirts, focus on designs that will look good on both dark and light shirts.
  - For mugs, think about both sides and the handle area.
  - For phone cases, consider how your design will fit around the cutouts for buttons and the camera.

- **File Specifications:** Ensure your designs are high resolution and meet the POD platform's file requirements (usually 300 DPI and a specific file format, like PNG with a transparent background).

- **Mockups:** Most POD platforms provide automatic mockup generators for your products. These mockups allow customers to see your designs in real-life context, such as a t-shirt being worn or a mug sitting on a table.

5. Set Your Pricing

- **Cost of Goods:** Each POD provider will have a base price for each product, which includes the printing cost. You'll need to mark up these prices to make a profit.

- **Pricing Strategy:** Consider the value of your designs and your target market's price tolerance. You can use competitors' prices as a benchmark but ensure you're adding enough margin to cover marketing costs and make a profit.

Tip: Some sellers use tiered pricing for different quantities or offer discounts for bulk orders, so keep this in mind.

6. Market Your Store

Once your store is set up and your designs are live, it's time to market your products. Here are some strategies:

- **Social Media:** Platforms like Instagram, Facebook, and Pinterest are great for visual products. Share your designs and create engaging posts around them (e.g., design inspirations, customer testimonials, limited-time offers).

- **Email Marketing:** Build an email list to send updates about new designs, promotions, and sales. Use tools like Mailchimp or Klaviyo to automate your email campaigns.

- **Influencer Marketing:** Collaborate with influencers in your niche to help spread the word about your products. Micro-influencers are often more cost-effective and engaged with their audience.

- **Paid Ads:** Running targeted ads on social media or Google can help drive traffic to your store. Focus on ads that highlight your best-selling or seasonal designs.

7. Optimize for SEO

- **Product Descriptions:** Write clear, keyword-optimized product descriptions to improve search engine visibility. Include relevant keywords like "custom t-shirt," "funny mug," or "personalized phone case."

- **Blog or Content Marketing:** Start a blog or create content around your niche. For example, if you're selling custom fitness apparel, write articles on fitness trends, workout tips, or activewear guides.

8. Monitor, Scale, and Optimize

- **Track Analytics:** Use tools like Google Analytics and the analytics provided by your POD platform to track sales, traffic, and customer behavior. This data will help you understand what's working and what needs improvement.

- **Expand Your Product Range:** Once you start making sales, consider adding new products like hoodies, tote bags, or posters to diversify your offerings.

- **Customer Service:** Provide excellent customer service, respond to inquiries promptly, and maintain a professional demeanor in all communications.

9. Automate and Streamline

As your business grows, look for ways to automate your processes:

- **Email automation** for customer follow-ups, abandoned cart reminders, and promotions.

- **Social media scheduling tools** (like Buffer or Hootsuite) to keep your accounts active without spending too much time daily.

- **Outsource Design Work:** If you find design creation too time-consuming, you can hire freelance graphic designers to scale up your store's design offerings.

Final Thoughts

Starting a print-on-demand store is a relatively low-risk, low-investment way to enter the eCommerce world. By focusing on your niche, creating high-quality designs, choosing the right POD platform, and marketing effectively, you can build a successful business. The beauty of POD is that you don't have to worry about inventory management, production, or shipping—just focus on creating great designs and offering excellent customer service!

Chapter 56

Start a Crowdfunding Campaign

Starting a crowdfunding campaign for a product, service, or creative endeavor is an exciting way to bring your idea to life with the support of a community. Here's a step-by-step guide to help you launch a successful crowdfunding campaign, using platforms like Kickstarter, Indiegogo, or GoFundMe.

1. Define Your Vision and Set Clear Goals

Clarify your mission.

Before you launch a crowdfunding campaign, it's crucial to have a clear understanding of what you're trying to accomplish. Ask yourself:

- What problem is your product or service solving?

- Why is this project important to you, and why should it matter to others?

- What are the specific financial and creative goals you want to achieve?

Your goal should be concrete (e.g., raising $10,000 to fund a product prototype) and time-sensitive (e.g., a 30-day campaign). A well-defined goal helps your audience understand the purpose of your campaign and feel confident in supporting it.

2. Choose the Right Crowdfunding Platform

Select a platform that aligns with your project.

Popular crowdfunding platforms include:

- **Kickstarter**: Best for creative projects like art, music, tech innovations, and products.

- **Indiegogo:** Offers both fixed and flexible funding options, and is great for tech, gadgets, and innovations.

- **GoFundMe:** Ideal for personal causes, medical expenses, or charitable projects.

Consider the fees, audience, and focus of each platform before deciding. Kickstarter is typically all-or-nothing (if you don't meet your goal, you get nothing), while Indiegogo offers both flexible and fixed funding models.

3. Craft a Compelling Story

Tell your story.

People contribute to crowdfunding campaigns because they believe in the story behind the project. Your campaign page should clearly convey:

- **What** your project is and how it will impact people.

- **Why** you are passionate about the project.

- **How** the funds will be used.

Make it personal and engaging. Use a conversational tone and include visuals such as sketches, photos, or videos to help bring your project to life.

4. Set Realistic Funding Goals and Reward Tiers

Determine your funding needs.

Be realistic about how much money you need to reach your goal. Factor in production costs, platform fees (usually 5%–10%), shipping, and marketing.

Create compelling reward tiers.

Offer a range of reward options for backers, such as:

- A thank-you message for small donations.

- Early-bird discounts on products for larger pledges.

- Exclusive behind-the-scenes access or limited-edition items for your highest supporters.

Keep in mind that your reward tiers should reflect the value of what you're offering and make it easy for backers to feel like they're part of something special.

5. Create a High-Quality Campaign Video

Capture attention with a compelling video.

A well-made campaign video is one of the most effective ways to connect with potential backers. Make sure to:

- Keep it short (around 1–3 minutes).

- Explain who you are, what you're creating, and why people should care.

- Show off prototypes, sketches, or the process behind your project.

- Include a call to action (e.g., "Back our campaign today and help bring this idea to life!").

Tip: People are more likely to donate if they feel personally connected to you. Be authentic, and show your passion!

6. Plan and Launch a Marketing Strategy

Build momentum before you launch.

Start promoting your campaign well before it goes live. Create a mailing list, engage with your social media followers, and tease your project to build interest.

Once your campaign is live:

- Use **social media** platforms to drive traffic (Facebook, Instagram, TikTok, Twitter, etc.).

- Reach out to **influencers** or bloggers in your niche who can help spread the word.

- Engage with your backers by responding to questions and comments promptly.

- Consider **paid ads** (if within your budget) to help reach a wider audience.

Tip: Don't forget to update your backers regularly on the progress of the campaign, and offer sneak peeks or exciting updates to maintain engagement.

7. Leverage Backers as Advocates

Encourage sharing and word-of-mouth marketing.

Encourage your backers to share the campaign with their networks. Offer special incentives for people who refer others to your campaign, such as exclusive rewards or shout-outs.

Engage with backers on social media and within the campaign's comment section. Show appreciation for their support, and remind them of the impact their contributions are having.

8. Prepare for Post-Campaign Fulfillment

Set expectations for delivery.

Once your campaign ends, be transparent about when backers can expect their rewards. Stay on top of production and shipping timelines, and provide frequent updates. Communicate any delays early to maintain trust.

Remember that the work doesn't stop once the campaign is funded. You'll need to follow through on your promises, deliver products, and maintain a good relationship with your backers, as they could be future customers or advocates.

9. Evaluate and Iterate

Reflect on what worked and what didn't.

After your campaign concludes, take time to analyze your performance. Consider what aspects of your campaign were most successful and which areas need improvement. If you plan to run another campaign in the future, these insights will help you make it even better.

Final Thoughts

Starting a crowdfunding campaign is a powerful way to turn your creative idea or business venture into reality. By crafting a compelling story, offering valuable rewards, building a strong marketing plan, and engaging with your backers, you'll be on your way to launching a successful campaign. With determination, transparency, and the support of your community, you can bring your vision to life.

Chapter 57

Venture into Angel Investing

Starting a venture into angel investing can be an exciting and potentially rewarding way to grow your wealth while supporting innovative entrepreneurs. If you have capital to invest and want to get started with early-stage startups, equity crowdfunding platforms are an excellent place to begin. Here's a guide to help you kick off your angel investing journey:

1. Understand Angel Investing and the Risks Involved

Before diving into the world of angel investing, it's crucial to understand what it entails:

- **Angel Investing Defined:** Angel investing involves providing financial support to early-stage startups or entrepreneurs in exchange for equity (ownership) in the company. As an angel investor, you are betting on the potential success of a startup and helping them get off the ground in return for a potential high return if the company grows and becomes successful.

- **Risks:** Early-stage startups have a high failure rate, and investing in them can be risky. Many startups won't succeed, and you could lose your investment. However, successful startups can offer substantial returns, often far exceeding traditional investments.

2. Do Your Research

Before you start investing, it's essential to research the startup ecosystem and understand the types of businesses that tend to do well. Here are some tips:

- **Industry Trends:** Research emerging industries and markets to find startups that have high growth potential. Tech, biotech, clean energy, and fintech are popular areas, but opportunities exist across various sectors.

- **Startup Stage:** Early-stage startups can range from pre-seed to Series A funding rounds. Pre-seed and seed-stage companies carry higher risk but can offer the highest potential returns.

- **Founders:** Investigate the backgrounds of the founders. Successful entrepreneurs often have a track record of building successful companies or experience in the industry they're entering.

3. Select the Right Equity Crowdfunding Platform

Equity crowdfunding platforms make it easy for individual investors to participate in angel investing by pooling funds with other investors to invest in startups. Some popular platforms include:

- SeedInvest

- WeFunder

- Republic

- StartEngine

- Crowdcube (UK-based)

When choosing a platform, consider the following:

- **Platform Reputation:** Look for platforms with a strong track record of vetting startups and protecting investors.

- **Types of Startups:** Some platforms specialize in specific industries or business stages, so choose a platform that aligns with your investment interests.

- **Fees and Terms:** Review the fee structure and investment terms on each platform. Some platforms charge administrative fees, while others may take a commission from successful exits.

- **Regulatory Compliance:** Ensure the platform is compliant with financial regulations, such as those established by the SEC in the U.S. or equivalent bodies in other countries.

4. Build Your Portfolio

As a first-time angel investor, it's important to diversify your investments. Instead of putting all your capital into a single startup, consider spreading your investments across multiple businesses in different industries and stages. This reduces risk while maximizing your exposure to potential high-growth opportunities.

- **Diversification:** Angel investors typically invest in 5-10 startups at a time, often investing small amounts into each. This approach spreads the risk and increases the likelihood that one of your investments will succeed.

- **Investment Amounts:** Many equity crowdfunding platforms allow you to start with small investments (e.g., $1,000 to $10,000 per company). As you gain experience and confidence, you can increase your investments.

5. Due Diligence

One of the most important parts of angel investing is conducting thorough due diligence on each startup you're considering investing in. This includes:

- **Business Model:** Does the company have a clear business model and growth plan? Is there a strong path to profitability?

- **Financial Health:** Review their financial projections, balance sheets, and funding needs. Do they have enough runway to hit key milestones?

- **Market Opportunity:** Does the startup solve a real problem in a growing market?

- **Management Team:** Assess the skills and experience of the leadership team. Strong founders with industry experience are often a key indicator of potential success.

- **Exit Strategy:** Understand the exit strategy for each startup. Will there be an acquisition, IPO, or other opportunities to realize returns?

6. Invest and Monitor Your Portfolio

Once you've made your investments, it's essential to stay engaged and monitor the performance of your portfolio. While you won't be involved in day-to-day operations, many equity crowdfunding platforms allow you to follow updates on the startups, such as progress reports, financial updates, and key milestones.

- **Engagement:** Stay connected with founders and network with other investors. Many platforms offer communication tools or investor updates, so you can track the company's progress and ask questions.

- **Follow-on Investments:** As companies grow, they may go through additional funding rounds. Sometimes, existing investors are given the opportunity to participate in follow-on investments to maintain or increase their ownership percentage.

7. Be Patient and Prepare for Long-Term Investment

Angel investing typically requires a long-term outlook. Most early-stage startups take several years to reach significant milestones or exits. Be prepared for the possibility that your investments may not yield returns for several years, and in some cases, may not result in any returns at all.

- **Exit Strategies:** Depending on the success of the startup, you may receive returns through an acquisition, an IPO, or secondary market sales of shares. However, not every investment will have a successful exit, so it's crucial to be patient and realistic about the potential for failure.

8. Continue Learning and Networking

Angel investing is a dynamic field, and the best investors are those who continuously learn and improve their strategies. Engage with other angel investors, attend industry conferences, and read books or follow blogs related to startup investing. You'll continue to refine your approach and make better-informed investment decisions as you gain more experience.

Final Thoughts

Angel investing can be a powerful way to diversify your portfolio while supporting innovation and entrepreneurship. By starting on equity crowdfunding platforms, you can gain exposure to early-stage startups with relatively low investment amounts, while also mitigating some risks through diversification. However, success in angel investing requires patience, a willingness to take calculated risks, and a commitment to ongoing learning.

If you're ready to invest, remember that it's not just about the money—it's about being part of the entrepreneurial journey and potentially making a significant impact on the startup ecosystem.

Chapter 58

Start a Vending Machine Business

Starting a vending machine business can be a great way to generate passive income by leveraging high-traffic locations and providing convenient snack and drink options. Here's a step-by-step guide to help you start your vending machine business:

1. Research the Vending Machine Industry

- Understand the types of vending machines available (e.g., snack, beverage, healthy food, or even combination machines).

- Research industry trends, like the shift toward healthier snack options, contactless payment systems, and eco-friendly machines.

- Learn about your target market—whether it's commuters, students, office workers, or gym-goers—and understand their preferences.

2. Create a Business Plan

- **Investment Plan:** Determine your startup costs, including the cost of purchasing vending machines, stocking products, and maintenance.

- **Revenue Projections:** Estimate how much revenue you can expect from each machine based on location and the products you offer.

- **Marketing Strategy:** Develop a plan for negotiating with location owners and keeping machines stocked and well-maintained.

- **Business Structure:** Decide whether you will operate as a sole proprietorship, LLC, or corporation.

3. Legal Considerations and Permits

- Obtain any necessary permits or licenses for operating a vending business in your state or city.

- Research local regulations regarding vending operations, such as health and safety codes, tax requirements, and placement restrictions.

- Consider setting up a legal entity, like an LLC, for liability protection and tax purposes.

4. Find the Right Vending Machines

- **New vs. Used Machines:** Decide whether to buy new or refurbished vending machines. New machines are more expensive but tend to have fewer maintenance issues. Used machines are more affordable but may require more upkeep.

- **Features to Consider:** Look for machines with modern payment systems (e.g., credit/debit card readers, mobile payment options) and energy-efficient designs.

- **Machine Types:** Select the types of vending machines that align with your target market (e.g., snack machines, soda machines, healthy options, or even non-food items like masks or toiletries).

5. Scout High-Traffic Locations

- Location is key to a successful vending machine business. High-traffic areas such as:
  - Office buildings
  - Schools and universities
  - Hospitals or medical centers
  - Airports or train stations
  - Gyms or fitness centers
- Approach business owners or property managers to negotiate placement agreements. Be prepared to offer them a share of the revenue in exchange for allowing you to place machines on their property.
- Choose locations that have consistent foot traffic and are easily accessible.

6. Stock the Machines with Popular Products

- Offer a variety of snacks and drinks that cater to different tastes and dietary preferences. Popular options include:
  - Chips, candy bars, and cookies for traditional snack machines.
  - Healthy snacks like granola bars, fruit snacks, and protein bars for health-conscious customers.
  - Bottled water, soda, energy drinks, and juice for beverage machines.
- Keep in mind the demographic of each location to ensure the products appeal to your customers.

7. Set Your Prices

- Price your products competitively while ensuring you cover the cost of goods and make a reasonable profit.
- Factor in the location's clientele and adjust prices based on demand. For example, vending machines in busy office buildings may be able to charge a bit more for convenience.
- Keep in mind additional costs, such as maintenance, refills, and potential fees for machine placement.

8. Maintain and Restock Machines Regularly

- One of the keys to a successful vending business is maintaining your machines. Regularly check that machines are in good working order, and repair any mechanical issues promptly.

- Keep machines stocked with fresh products. Frequent restocking is essential to maintaining customer satisfaction and ensuring the machine stays profitable.

   - Pay attention to expiration dates and replace expired products to avoid complaints.

9. Monitor Your Performance and Optimize

   - Use machine data (if available) to track which products are selling the most and which are underperforming.

   - Consider adjusting the product mix based on customer preferences and sales data. If certain items aren't selling well, replace them with more popular options.

   - As your business grows, you may want to expand to more locations or add additional machines to your existing sites.

10. Scale Your Business

   - Once you've established your vending machine business and have a reliable system in place, look for opportunities to expand.

   - Seek out new, profitable locations and continue to build your network with property owners or managers.

   - You can also diversify your vending options by offering specialized machines, such as those with fresh food, coffee, or even non-food products (e.g., electronics, accessories, or office supplies).

Final Thoughts

The vending machine business offers a flexible and relatively low-maintenance way to generate passive income. Success depends on selecting the right locations, offering appealing products, and maintaining your machines. By starting small and scaling as you gain experience, you can build a profitable business that requires minimal day-to-day effort once it's up and running.

Final Thoughts

As we wrap up this journey, I hope the insights and strategies shared in this book empower you to take charge of your financial future. The world is constantly changing, and the opportunities to make money whether through leveraging skills, resources, or simply staying adaptable are abundant.

The methods outlined in these chapters are designed to be accessible to anyone, regardless of prior experience or capital. Some require minimal upfront investment, while others rely more on your dedication and willingness to learn. The key is applying the knowledge you've gained and maintaining the determination to follow through on your goals.

Remember, success is not defined by how quickly you get there but by your commitment to the process. Every step you take toward building your future is progress, and over time, those efforts will compound into real results. The economy may change, but those who stay ahead of the curve and adapt will continue to thrive.

This book is a resource guide to help you navigate the evolving landscape of personal finance, entrepreneurship, and investment opportunities. It is not, however, intended as investment advice, and we cannot take responsibility for any financial outcomes you experience from implementing these ideas. Every decision you make should be informed and considered carefully, with an understanding that risks are inherent in any endeavour.

Ultimately, the knowledge shared here is meant to spark action. You now have a toolkit for moving forward, for creating a better financial future, and for capitalizing on the opportunities that lie ahead. The road may not always be smooth, but with persistence and the right mindset, your success is within reach.

Thank you for trusting me to guide you through this process. I believe in your ability to take these ideas and turn them into reality. The future is yours to shape, Start today and make it happen.

www.ingramcontent.com/pod-product-compliance
Lightning Source LLC
Chambersburg PA
CBHW071531220526
45469CB00003B/726